HUMAN RESOURCES IN THE GIG ECONOMY

Navigating the Future World of Work

Eugene George A.

ABOUT THE AUTHOR

Eugene George A., the architect behind the illuminating journey within "HUMAN RESOURCES IN THE GIG ECONOMY: Navigating the Future World of Work," is no ordinary author. His narrative prowess transcends the conventional, propelling readers into a realm where words are not just ink on paper but living entities, shaping the very fabric of the future workplace.

Draped in the cloak of curiosity and armed with a pen that doubles as a visionary compass, Eugene takes his readers on an exhilarating adventure through the dynamic landscapes of human resources and the gig economy. A maestro of words, he orchestrates a symphony where traditional paradigms dance with the rhythm of innovation, and the workforce transforms into a tapestry of possibilities.

Eugene George A. isn't just an author; he's a trailblazer in the unexplored territories of work dynamics. His narrative style is a fusion of insight and inspiration, inviting readers to not just consume information but to actively participate in the evolution of the professional landscape. In a world where the gig economy's pulse beats louder every day, Eugene stands as a guide, mentor, and visionary, leading the way with a narrative that sparks curiosity, ignites passion, and unlocks the doors to the future world of work.

Prepare to be captivated by Eugene George A.'s storytelling magic—a literary virtuoso shaping the future of work one word at a time. Buckle up, for the journey he unfolds isn't just about navigating the gig economy; it's an expedition into the uncharted territories of our professional destinies. The story is written, and Eugene George A. is the author whose narrative promises to linger in the minds of readers, leaving an indelible mark on the evolving tale of work in the gig era.

TABLE OF CONTENT

INTRODUCTION

In the bustling city of Workopolis, where the skyscrapers of tradition met the ever-shifting clouds of innovation, a seasoned storyteller named Eugene George A. emerged. Armed with a pen that doubled as a compass, he embarked on a literary journey to unravel the tales of the gig economy—those enigmatic byways where traditional norms danced with the rhythm of change.

Picture this: a world where the predictable 9-to-5 rhythms were replaced by a symphony of flexibility, where the cubicles of yesteryear made way for virtual realms, and where the protagonists of this story weren't just employees but gig workers, wielding skills as their swords and adaptability as their shields.

As the ink of Eugene's pen touched the pages, the narrative unfolded—a tapestry of challenges, opportunities, and the relentless spirit of HR professionals navigating this brave new world of work. In "Human Resource in the Gig Economy: Navigating the Future World of Work," Eugene beckoned readers to join him on an expedition through the uncharted territories of the professional landscape.

Through the corridors of talent acquisition, across the bridges of agile leadership, and into the heart of innovative HR practices, Eugene crafted a tale that wasn't just a guide but an adventure—a call to action for HR leaders to be the architects of change, the navigators of flexibility, and the champions of the human spirit in the gig era.

So, dear reader, buckle up as Eugene George A. invites you to immerse yourself in this story, where the future of work isn't just a destination—it's a dynamic journey waiting to be explored. Grab your compass, unfold the map, and let the adventure begin in "Human Resource in the Gig Economy: Navigating the Future World of Work." After all, every great story starts with a storyteller, and Eugene has just opened the door to a world where the tales of the gig economy are waiting to be written.

1. NAVIGATING THE GIG ECONOMY: A STRATEGIC GUIDE FOR HR PROFESSIONALS

Welcome to the dynamic world of work where the gig economy isn't just a trend; it's a thriving ecosystem reshaping the very fabric of how we define careers. If you're an HR professional, consider this your backstage pass to the gig economy—a realm where agility, innovation, and collaboration take center stage. Buckle up as we embark on a strategic journey, navigating the twists and turns of gig work, and unraveling the secrets that will empower you to orchestrate a harmonious symphony of talent in this ever-evolving gig landscape. This is not just a guide; it's your compass in the exhilarating adventure of Navigating the Gig Economy. Let's dive in!

Adapting HR Policies to Harness the Power of Gig Workers

Adapting HR policies to embrace the potential of gig workers is a game-changer for modern businesses. In this rapidly evolving landscape, where traditional employment models are giving way to more flexible arrangements, HR professionals find themselves at the forefront of change.

Crafting policies that resonate with the gig economy involves a delicate balance. On one hand, there's a need to provide the autonomy and flexibility that gig workers seek. On the other, it's crucial to ensure a sense of belonging and alignment with the organization's goals.

Imagine designing policies that allow gig workers to seamlessly integrate into the company culture, even if their tenure is project-specific. It's about fostering a sense of community and shared values, despite the transient nature of their roles. Flexibility, communication, and mutual respect become the cornerstones of these policies.

Moreover, the gig economy thrives on diversity, with individuals bringing unique skills and perspectives to the table. HR policies must be inclusive, recognizing and appreciating the differences that each gig worker brings. Tailoring benefits packages to cater to diverse needs and preferences is a step towards building a robust and attractive gig workforce.

Embracing technology is another crucial aspect. HR policies need to accommodate the use of digital tools for seamless onboarding, communication, and performance tracking. Creating a tech-savvy environment ensures that gig workers feel connected and supported, even in virtual settings.

In essence, adapting HR policies for gig workers is about fostering an environment where flexibility and structure coexist harmoniously. It's recognizing that the gig economy isn't just a trend; it's a fundamental shift in the way we work. HR policies, as the backbone of any organization, have the power to either propel it forward into this new era or hold it back. It's an exciting challenge, an opportunity to redefine the employer-employee relationship, and ultimately, a step towards a more agile and inclusive future of work.

Building Agile Teams: Lessons from the Gig Economy

Building agile teams draws inspiration from the dynamic nature of the gig economy, where adaptability is key to success. In today's ever-evolving business landscape, traditional team structures are giving way to a more flexible and responsive approach. Here are some invaluable lessons we can glean from the gig economy to foster agility within our teams:

a). Embrace Diversity and Specialization:

In the gig economy, diversity isn't just a buzzword; it's a fundamental strength. Teams comprised of individuals with diverse skill sets and backgrounds bring a wealth of perspectives to the table. Much like assembling a gig workforce, building agile teams involves recognizing and leveraging the unique strengths and specializations of each team member.

b). Promote a Culture of Continuous Learning:

Gig workers thrive on adaptability, constantly upskilling to stay relevant. Applying this principle to team dynamics means fostering a culture of continuous learning. Encourage team members to explore new skills, share knowledge, and be open to trying different roles within the team. A learning-centric culture fuels innovation and ensures teams remain agile in the face of change.

c). Prioritize Flexibility in Roles and Responsibilities:

One hallmark of the gig economy is the ability to take on diverse roles. Similarly, agile teams benefit from flexibility in roles and responsibilities. Team members should be equipped to pivot quickly, taking on tasks outside their traditional scope when needed. This flexibility ensures that teams can respond nimbly to shifting priorities and emerging challenges.

d). Leverage Technology for Collaboration:

The gig economy thrives on digital platforms that facilitate seamless communication and collaboration. Applying this lesson to building agile teams means leveraging technology to enhance communication and streamline collaboration. Whether it's project management tools, virtual communication platforms, or collaborative workspaces, technology plays a crucial role in keeping agile teams connected and productive.

e). Encourage Autonomy with Accountability:

Gig workers often operate with a high degree of autonomy, responsible for delivering results independently. Translating this to agile teams involves trusting team members to take ownership of their tasks while maintaining accountability for outcomes. Empower teams to make decisions at the project level, fostering a sense of ownership that fuels motivation and productivity.

f). Adapt Communication Styles:

Communication in the gig economy is often tailored to suit virtual and diverse work environments. Agile teams can benefit from adopting clear and adaptable communication styles. This includes embracing asynchronous communication when needed, leveraging video conferencing for a more personal touch, and ensuring transparency in team updates and decisions.

In essence, building agile teams draws inspiration from the gig economy's ability to thrive in a world of constant change. By embracing diversity, promoting continuous learning, prioritizing flexibility, leveraging technology, encouraging autonomy, and adapting communication styles, teams can navigate the complexities of the modern business landscape with agility and resilience.

Innovative Talent Acquisition in the Era of Freelancers

Navigating the landscape of talent acquisition in the era of freelancers requires a paradigm shift in traditional recruiting strategies. The rise of freelancers offers a pool of diverse and skilled professionals, and embracing innovation in talent acquisition is key to tapping into this dynamic workforce. Here are some insights into adopting an innovative approach:

a). Cultivate a Freelancer-Friendly Brand:

Just as companies strive to be attractive employers for full-time staff, cultivating a freelancer-friendly brand is crucial. Showcase your commitment to flexibility, project variety, and a supportive work environment. Highlighting successful freelance collaborations can serve as a powerful magnet for top-tier freelancers looking for engaging opportunities.

b). Leverage Freelance Platforms and Networks:

In the era of freelancers, online platforms and networks dedicated to freelance talent are treasure troves of potential collaborators. Incorporate these platforms into your talent acquisition strategy to connect with freelancers across diverse domains. Explore platforms that align with your industry, and actively engage with these communities to discover hidden talent gems.

c). Create Targeted Freelancer Personas:

Tailor your talent acquisition efforts by creating targeted freelancer personas. Understand the unique motivations, preferences, and expectations of freelancers in your industry. This insight enables you to craft personalized recruitment messages and offerings that resonate with the specific needs of freelance professionals.

d). Implement Agile Hiring Processes:

Freelancers are accustomed to quick decision-making and shorter recruitment cycles. To attract top freelance talent, streamline your hiring processes. Implement agile recruitment practices, from rapid application reviews to efficient interview processes. The goal is to provide a seamless experience that aligns with the fast-paced nature of freelance work.

e). Offer Project-Based Opportunities:

Freelancers thrive on project-based opportunities that allow them to showcase their skills and contribute meaningfully. When crafting job listings, emphasize the project's scope, objectives, and the impact freelancers can make. Clearly defined projects attract freelancers seeking tangible outcomes and a clear understanding of their role.

f). Foster a Culture of Flexibility:

Flexibility is a hallmark of freelancing. Signal to freelancers that your company values and supports flexible work arrangements. Whether it's remote work options, flexible hours, or project-based timelines, showcasing a commitment to adaptability will make your organization more appealing to freelancers seeking autonomy in their work.

g). Collaborate with Freelance Talent Agencies:

Partnering with freelance talent agencies or specialized recruiters can be a strategic move. These agencies often have a pool of pre-vetted freelancers with diverse skills.

By collaborating, you gain access to a curated talent pool, saving time in the recruitment process and ensuring a higher likelihood of finding the right fit for your projects.

h). *Emphasize a Results-Driven Approach:*

Freelancers are results-oriented professionals. In your talent acquisition messaging, emphasize a results-driven approach. Clearly articulate the goals and expected outcomes of the projects, showcasing your commitment to recognizing and rewarding freelancers based on their contributions and achievements.

Innovative talent acquisition in the era of freelancers revolves around understanding and adapting to the unique dynamics of the freelance workforce. By embracing flexibility, leveraging online platforms, and cultivating a freelancer-friendly brand, organizations can position themselves as attractive destinations for top freelance talent.

Fostering Engagement: HR Strategies for a Dispersed Gig Workforce

Creating a sense of connection and engagement in a dispersed gig workforce is both an art and a necessity for HR professionals navigating the contemporary world of work. Here are some human-centric strategies to foster engagement among your gig workers spread across diverse locations:

a). Virtual Onboarding with a Personal Touch:

Introduce a warm and personalized virtual onboarding process. Utilize video calls to introduce new gig workers to the team, provide an overview of the company culture, and ensure they feel a sense of belonging from day one. Sending a welcome package or personalized messages goes a long way in making them feel valued.

b). Regular Check-Ins Beyond Projects:

Establish a routine for regular check-ins that go beyond project updates. Use video calls or informal virtual coffee sessions to discuss their experiences, address concerns, and learn more about their goals. Building personal connections helps gig workers feel like integral members of the team rather than isolated contributors.

c). Create a Virtual Community Hub:

Develop a virtual community or platform where gig workers can connect, share experiences, and collaborate. This could be a dedicated space on your company's communication platform or a social hub where gig workers can engage in casual conversations, share insights, and celebrate achievements.

d). Recognition and Appreciation:

Acknowledge and appreciate the contributions of gig workers publicly. Whether through virtual shout-outs in team meetings or recognition on company-wide platforms, celebrating their efforts reinforces a sense of accomplishment and encourages continued dedication to the projects they undertake.

e). Facilitate Skill-Sharing Sessions:

Encourage a culture of knowledge-sharing among gig workers. Organize virtual sessions where they can showcase their expertise or learn from each other. This not only enhances their skills but also fosters a collaborative environment, even in a dispersed setting.

f). Offer Professional Development Opportunities:

Provide opportunities for professional growth and development. Whether through online courses, webinars, or mentorship programs, supporting gig workers in advancing their skills and careers reinforces their value to the organization.

g). Transparent Communication:

Maintain transparent communication regarding company updates, future projects, and changes. Clear communication helps gig workers understand their role in the broader context, fostering a sense of involvement and commitment to the company's mission.

h). Flexible Work Policies:

Embrace flexibility in work hours and project timelines. Recognize the unique circumstances of gig workers and provide autonomy in managing their schedules. This not only enhances work-life balance but also demonstrates trust in their ability to deliver results independently.

i). Employee Assistance Programs (EAPs):

Extend support through employee assistance programs that cater to the well-being of gig workers. Access to mental health resources, counseling services, and wellness initiatives contributes to their overall satisfaction and engagement.

j). Feedback and Performance Reviews:

Implement regular feedback mechanisms and performance reviews. Constructive feedback helps gig workers understand their impact and areas for improvement, fostering a continuous improvement mindset.

In essence, fostering engagement in a dispersed gig workforce is about creating a virtual environment where individuals feel connected, valued, and supported. By prioritizing personalized interactions, recognizing contributions, and providing opportunities for growth, HR professionals can build a culture that transcends physical boundaries and enhances the overall engagement of gig workers.

2. GIG WORK REVOLUTION: HR'S ROLE IN THE FUTURE OF EMPLOYMENT

Step into the spotlight, HR trailblazers, because the stage is set for a revolution—a revolution in the way we define, embrace, and champion work. In this ever-evolving narrative of employment, you, the HR professionals, are not just spectators; you are the architects shaping the future. Welcome to the Work Revolution, where the norms are rewritten, possibilities are limitless, and HR's role is pivotal. Get ready to be the authors of a new employment saga, because this isn't just about adapting to change; it's about steering the course of a future where work isn't just a task; it's a journey of innovation, growth, and boundless potential. The future of employment awaits, and HR, you're leading the charge!

Revolutionizing Recruitment: Attracting and Retaining Gig Talent

Revolutionizing recruitment to attract and retain gig talent is a journey that demands a fresh perspective and a genuine understanding of the evolving dynamics in the workforce. Here are some human-centric strategies to spark a revolution in how we bring in and keep top-notch gig professionals:

a). Craft Authentic and Compelling Job Listings:

Begin by ditching the cookie-cutter job descriptions. Craft listings that tell a story about the project, your company culture, and the exciting challenges ahead. Gig workers are drawn to roles that resonate with them on a personal and professional level.

b). Showcase Your Company Culture:

Highlighting your company culture is more than just a trend; it's a powerful recruitment tool. Use social media, company blogs, or even virtual office tours to showcase the environment, values, and the human side of your organization. This transparency helps gig workers assess cultural fit and envision themselves as part of the team.

c). Flexibility is Key:

Recognize that flexibility is a cornerstone of gig work. Be transparent about flexible work arrangements, project timelines, and remote possibilities. A commitment to flexibility is not just attractive but also instrumental in retaining gig talent in the long run.

d). Build a Gig Talent Community:

Create a talent community specifically for gig workers. Engage with them on social media, host virtual meetups, and foster a sense of belonging. A community-centric approach not only attracts gig talent but also establishes a network where professionals can connect and share insights.

e). Streamline the Application Process:

Simplify the application and onboarding processes. Gig workers appreciate efficiency. Cumbersome paperwork and lengthy procedures can be deterrents. A streamlined process signals that you respect their time and value their contributions.

f). Provide Clear Project Outcomes:

When recruiting for gig roles, be crystal clear about project outcomes and expectations. Gig workers are often results-driven, and knowing the tangible impact of their work is a powerful motivator. Clearly defined expectations also set the stage for a successful collaboration.

g). Facilitate Networking Opportunities:

Foster networking opportunities for gig workers within your organization. Whether through virtual events, team-building activities, or mentorship programs, creating avenues for professional connections contributes to a sense of community and professional growth.

h). Offer Competitive Compensation and Benefits:

Recognize the value that gig workers bring to your projects by offering competitive compensation. Additionally, consider providing benefits such as access to training programs, professional development opportunities, and even limited access to company perks to enhance their overall experience.

i). Feedback is a Two-Way Street:

Create an environment that encourages open feedback. Gig workers, like any other employees, appreciate constructive feedback on their work. Simultaneously, be open to receiving feedback on the recruitment and project processes to continually refine and improve the experience or everyone involved.

j). Prioritize Retention Strategies:

Retention doesn't end with recruitment; it's an ongoing effort. Implement strategies to keep gig talent engaged beyond their initial project. This could include offering them first dibs on new opportunities, recognizing their contributions, and even considering them for more permanent roles if the fit is right.

Revolutionizing recruitment for gig talent is about embracing the unique nature of this workforce and creating an environment that speaks to their aspirations, values, and expectations. By putting people at the center of your recruitment strategy, you not only attract top-tier gig talent but also build a reputation as an employer of choice in the gig economy.

Embracing Change: HR Leadership in the Gig Economy Era

Navigating the gig economy era demands a paradigm shift in HR leadership, where embracing change becomes not just a strategy but a way of life. Here's a human-centered perspective on how HR leaders can steer the ship through the currents of change in the gig economy era:

a). Cultivate an Adaptive Mindset:

In the gig economy, change is constant. HR leaders must cultivate an adaptive mindset that embraces uncertainty and is ready to pivot at a moment's notice. Instead of being afraid of change, see it as an opportunity for growth and innovation.

b). Empower and Trust Your Team:

Empower your HR team to take ownership of change initiatives. Trust is the glue that binds a team together, especially in times of transformation. Encourage autonomy, celebrate ideas, and foster an environment where team members feel confident taking calculated risks.

c). Invest in Continuous Learning:

The gig economy thrives on continuous learning, and HR leaders should set the example. Invest in ongoing training and development for your team, ensuring they stay ahead of industry trends, technological advancements, and changes in the employment landscape.

d). Facilitate Open Communication:

Change often breeds uncertainty, and open communication is the antidote. Keep channels of communication wide open, transparently sharing the reasons behind changes, the expected outcomes, and how it aligns with the organization's overarching goals. This transparency builds trust and reduces anxiety among the HR team.

e). Build a Culture of Resilience:

Resilience is a cornerstone of successful HR leadership in the gig economy era. Acknowledge challenges, learn from setbacks, and instill a sense of resilience within the team. This resilience becomes a guiding force, enabling HR professionals to adapt and overcome obstacles in the face of change.

f). Embrace Technology as an Enabler:

Technology is a powerful enabler in the gig economy landscape. HR leaders should embrace and leverage technology to streamline processes, enhance communication, and facilitate remote collaboration. This tech-savvy approach not only improves efficiency but also positions the HR team as forward-thinking leaders.

g). Foster a Collaborative Ecosystem:

In the gig economy, collaboration extends beyond traditional boundaries. HR leaders should foster a collaborative ecosystem that includes internal teams, freelancers, and external partners. Building bridges between these diverse contributors enhances agility and innovation.

h). Prioritize Employee Well-being:

Amidst change, prioritize the well-being of your HR team. The gig economy can bring about heightened workloads and increased stress. Implement initiatives that promote work-life balance, mental health support, and a culture of well-being within the HR department.

i). Adapt Talent Management Strategies:

Traditional talent management strategies may not align with the fluidity of the gig economy. HR leaders should adapt strategies to attract, engage, and retain gig workers. This may include revisiting performance management processes, offering flexible arrangements, and emphasizing project-based outcomes.

j). Lead by Example:

HR leaders serve as beacons of guidance. Lead by example in embracing change. Demonstrate a positive attitude, a willingness to learn, and an openness to experimentation. Your genuine commitment to navigating the challenges of the gig economy era will inspire confidence and resilience in your HR team.

In the era of the gig economy, HR leadership is not just about managing change; it's about championing it. By fostering a culture of adaptability, investing in continuous learning, and prioritizing the well-being of the HR team, leaders can navigate the complexities of the gig economy with grace and resilience.

Creating a Gig-Ready Work Culture: HR's Pivotal Role

Building a work culture that's primed for the gig economy requires a thoughtful and people-centric approach, with HR playing a pivotal role in steering the ship. Let's dive into the human side of creating a gig-ready work culture and the crucial role HR professionals play in this transformative journey:

a). Understanding the Gig Mindset:

To create a gig-ready culture, HR needs to get into the minds of gig workers. Understand their motivations, aspirations, and what they value in their work. This understanding forms the foundation for crafting policies and practices that resonate with the gig mindset.

b). Flexible Policies and Autonomy:

Flexibility is the heartbeat of the gig economy. HR plays a central role in crafting policies that allow for adaptability. This involves reimagining traditional structures to offer flexible work hours, remote options, and a level of autonomy that empowers gig workers to excel on their terms.

c). Clear Communication Channels:

Communication is the glue that holds a gig-ready culture together. HR needs to establish clear and open channels for communication, ensuring that gig workers are not only informed but also feel connected to the larger mission and values of the organization. Regular updates, virtual town halls, and interactive platforms can facilitate this connection.

d). Inclusive Onboarding Processes:

The onboarding experience sets the tone for a gig worker's journey. HR should design onboarding processes that are inclusive, informative, and imbued with the company's culture. Virtual welcome sessions, comprehensive resource kits, and mentorship programs can make gig workers feel like integral parts of the team from day one.

e). Recognition and Appreciation:

Gig workers thrive on recognition for their contributions. HR can implement systems for acknowledging achievements, whether big or small. This could be through virtual applause in team meetings, shout-outs on company-wide platforms, or even personalized thank-you notes. Feeling valued is a powerful motivator.

f). Opportunities for Skill Development:

HR should pave the way for continuous learning and development. Offering gig workers opportunities to enhance their skills not only contributes to their professional growth but also aligns with the gig ethos of staying relevant in a rapidly changing landscape.

g). Cultivate a Collaborative Environment:

Collaboration is key in the gig-ready world. HR should foster an environment where gig workers seamlessly collaborate with full-time employees, creating a unified team spirit. This could involve virtual team-building activities, cross-functional projects, and encouraging knowledge-sharing sessions.

h). Transparent Performance Feedback:

Establish transparent feedback mechanisms. Gig workers, like everyone else, appreciate constructive feedback. HR's role is to ensure that performance evaluations are clear, constructive, and provide a roadmap for improvement. Regular check-ins contribute to a sense of direction and purpose.

i). Provide Accessible Resources:

HR should ensure that gig workers have easy access to the resources they need to excel. Whether it's virtual tools, training materials, or support channels, a gig-ready culture is one where resources are readily available, eliminating unnecessary hurdles.

j). Caring for Well-being:

The well-being of gig workers is as important as any other employee. HR professionals should implement initiatives that address mental health, stress management, and overall well-being. This could include access to wellness programs, mental health resources, and supportive communities.

In essence, creating a gig-ready work culture is about aligning organizational practices with the expectations and preferences of gig workers. HR's role is not just administrative; it's about crafting an inclusive and dynamic environment where gig workers can thrive, contribute meaningfully, and feel a genuine sense of belonging.

Performance Management in a Gig-Driven World: Best Practices

In a world driven by gig work, redefining performance management is not just a necessity; it's an art that HR professionals need to master. Here's a human touch on some best practices for performance management in the gig-driven landscape:

a). Set Clear Expectations from the Start:

Transparency is the cornerstone of effective performance management. Clearly communicate expectations right from the start of the gig. Outline project goals, deliverables, and key performance indicators (KPIs). This clarity provides gig workers with a roadmap for success.

b). Frequent and Agile Feedback:

In the gig-driven world, the traditional annual performance review feels outdated. Embrace a culture of continuous feedback. Regular check-ins, project milestones celebrations, and constructive critiques ensure that gig workers are on the right track and feel recognized for their efforts.

c). Measure Outcomes, Not Just Output:

Shift the focus from mere output to meaningful outcomes. In the gig economy, it's not just about completing tasks but delivering tangible results. Define success metrics tied to the project's impact on the organization, allowing gig workers to see the broader significance of their contributions.

d). Recognition for Contributions:

Recognition holds immense value for gig workers. Whether it's a virtual round of applause in a team meeting, a shout-out on collaboration platforms, or even a personalized email acknowledging exceptional work, recognizing contributions fosters a sense of pride and motivation.

e). Customize Development Plans:

No two gig workers are the same. Tailor development plans to their individual goals and aspirations. Offer opportunities for upskilling in areas that align with their interests and the organization's needs. This personalized approach demonstrates a commitment to their professional growth.

f). Encourage Self-Reflection:

Empower gig workers to take ownership of their performance. Encourage self-reflection on completed projects, lessons learned, and areas for improvement. This introspective approach not only fosters a culture of continuous improvement but also positions gig workers as active contributors to their own success.

g). Embrace Technology for Evaluation:

Leverage technology for real-time performance evaluation. Implement tools that allow for the tracking of project milestones, collaboration, and the overall impact of gig workers. Technology not only streamlines the evaluation process but also provides concrete data for constructive discussions.

h). Facilitate Peer Recognition:

In a gig-driven world, peer recognition holds significant weight. Create avenues for gig workers to acknowledge and appreciate each other's contributions. Peer recognition programs contribute to a sense of community and shared success within the gig workforce.

i). Build a Feedback Culture:

Foster an environment where feedback is not just given by supervisors but is part of the overall culture. Encourage gig workers to provide feedback on processes, projects, and their overall experience. A two-way feedback culture contributes to a sense of collaboration and mutual growth.

j). Consider Long-Term Impact:

Recognize the long-term impact of gig workers on the organization. While individual gigs may be short-term, the relationships built and the knowledge gained have lasting effects. Consider these long-term implications when evaluating performance and determining opportunities for future collaborations.

In the gig-driven world, performance management is about more than just evaluating tasks; it's about recognizing and cultivating the unique contributions of gig workers. By embracing transparency, continuous feedback, and personalized development plans, HR professionals can create an environment where gig workers thrive, feel valued, and contribute meaningfully to the organization's success.

3. TALENT MANAGEMENT IN A GIG-DRIVEN WORLD: HR STRATEGIES UNVEILED

Hold onto your hats, HR visionaries, because the spotlight is shining on a new era of talent management—a realm where the traditional playbook gets a remix in the dynamic beats of the gig-driven world. Get ready to unveil a set of strategies that redefine how we nurture, engage, and amplify talent in this ever-evolving landscape. It's not just about managing; it's about orchestrating a symphony where gig workers take center stage. Welcome to the unveiling of Talent Management in a Gig-Driven World, where HR strategies aren't just revealed; they're revolutionized. Let's dive into the rhythm of innovation and shape the future of talent management together!

Strategic Talent Pools: Managing a Diverse Gig Workforce

Building and managing a diverse gig workforce involves more than just recruitment; it's a strategic endeavor that requires thoughtful planning and ongoing nurturing. Here's a human-centric take on cultivating and overseeing strategic talent pools in the dynamic realm of gig work:

a). *Understanding Diverse Skill Sets:*

Embrace the diversity within the gig workforce by understanding the unique skill sets each individual brings to the table. Recognize that gig workers aren't a one-size-fits-all solution; they're a mosaic of talents waiting to be strategically integrated into your talent pool.

b). *Strategic Planning for Varied Projects:*

Gig work often involves a multitude of projects with different requirements. Develop a strategic plan for talent acquisition that aligns with the diverse needs of these projects. This might involve creating specialized talent pools based on skills, project types, or industry expertise.

c). Cultivate Relationship Building:

In the world of gig work, relationships matter. Cultivate meaningful connections with gig workers even before a project begins. Establishing rapport creates a sense of loyalty and encourages gig workers to return for future opportunities, contributing to the continuity and stability of your talent pool.

d). Foster Inclusivity and Diversity:

Diverse perspectives fuel innovation. Actively seek out gig workers from various backgrounds, cultures, and experiences. Fostering an inclusive environment not only enriches the talent pool but also brings fresh insights and creativity to each project.

e). Tailor Communication for Engagement:

Effective communication is the linchpin of managing a diverse gig workforce. Tailor your communication strategies to engage with gig workers in ways that resonate with them. Whether it's through virtual meetups, personalized messages, or sharing success stories, effective communication builds a sense of community.

f). Prioritize Fair Compensation:

Fair compensation is a cornerstone of talent retention in the gig economy. Ensure that your compensation structures are competitive and reflective of the value gig workers bring. Fair treatment fosters a positive relationship and encourages gig workers to commit to long-term collaborations.

g). Create a Virtual Community Hub:

Establish a virtual community hub where gig workers can connect, share experiences, and collaborate. This digital space becomes a central point for communication, resource sharing, and building a sense of camaraderie among diverse gig professionals.

h). Implement Robust Talent Management Systems:

Invest in robust talent management systems that facilitate the tracking and assessment of gig workers. These systems can help identify high-performing individuals, track skill development, and streamline the process of matching the right talent with the right projects.

i). Provide Professional Development Opportunities:

Support the growth and development of gig workers. Offer opportunities for professional development, whether through training programs, mentorship initiatives, or access to industry events. This investment not only enhances individual skills but also contributes to the overall strength of your talent pool.

j). Proactive Succession Planning:

Anticipate future needs by engaging in proactive succession planning. Identify key roles and skills required for upcoming projects and ensure that your talent pool is primed with individuals who can seamlessly step into these positions when needed.

In managing a diverse gig workforce, the key lies in treating each gig worker as a valued individual while strategically aligning their skills with the evolving needs of your projects. By embracing diversity, fostering relationships, and creating an environment of continuous growth, you're not just managing a talent pool; you're nurturing a community of dynamic contributors.

Succession Planning in the Gig Era: Nurturing Future Leaders

Navigating succession planning in the gig era is a unique challenge that demands a shift in traditional approaches. Here's a human-centric perspective on how to nurture future leaders in a landscape dominated by gig work:

a). Identifying Leadership Potential:

In the gig era, leadership potential may not follow the traditional hierarchical path. Look beyond job titles and tenure. Identify individuals who consistently demonstrate leadership qualities, take initiative, and contribute significantly to projects. Potential leaders may emerge from unexpected corners of your diverse gig workforce.

b). Fostering a Growth Mindset:

Encourage a growth mindset within your gig workforce. Actively support and promote a culture that values continuous learning and development. Future leaders in the gig era are those who embrace challenges, seek opportunities for growth, and adapt to evolving landscapes.

c). Tailoring Development Plans:

Recognize that one-size-fits-all development plans may not be effective in the gig era. Tailor development plans to align with the aspirations and unique skills of individual gig workers. Provide opportunities for skill enhancement, mentorship, and exposure to different projects that foster leadership qualities.

d). Encouraging Mentorship and Knowledge Transfer:

Mentorship is a powerful tool for grooming future leaders. Facilitate mentorship programs within your gig workforce, connecting experienced individuals with those eager to learn. This knowledge transfer not only enhances skillsets but also builds a sense of community and shared success.

e). Building Collaborative Networks:

Future leaders in the gig era thrive on collaboration. Foster networks that encourage gig workers to share insights, collaborate on projects, and learn from each other. Building a collaborative ecosystem contributes to the development of leaders who understand the value of teamwork and collective success.

f).Recognizing and Rewarding Leadership Traits:

Acknowledge and reward gig workers who exhibit leadership traits. Recognition, whether through virtual applause in team meetings or public appreciation on company platforms, reinforces the importance of leadership qualities and motivates others to step into leadership roles.

g). Aligning Projects with Leadership Development:

Strategically align projects with leadership development goals. Identify projects that offer opportunities for gig workers to take on leadership responsibilities, make decisions, and showcase their ability to guide and inspire others. Practical leadership experiences contribute significantly to development.

h). Emphasizing Emotional Intelligence:

Leadership in the gig era is not just about technical skills; it requires emotional intelligence. Emphasize the importance of understanding and navigating emotions in the workplace. Future leaders should be adept at fostering positive team dynamics, resolving conflicts, and empathizing with diverse perspectives.

i). Creating Pathways for Advancement:

Establish clear pathways for advancement within your gig workforce. Communicate the opportunities for growth and leadership roles, providing a roadmap for ambitious gig workers. Clarity on career progression motivates individuals to invest in their development and aspire to leadership positions.

j). Embracing a Leadership Mindset:

Instill a leadership mindset within your gig workforce. Encourage individuals to view their contributions not just as tasks but as valuable contributions to the overall success of the organization. Cultivating a sense of ownership and responsibility fosters a leadership mindset among gig workers.

In the gig era, the concept of leadership is evolving, and succession planning requires adaptability and innovation. By recognizing potential leaders, fostering growth mindsets, and creating environments that value collaboration and emotional intelligence, organizations can nurture future leaders who thrive in the dynamic landscape of gig work.

HR's Guide to Skills Development: Empowering Gig Workers

Empowering gig workers through skills development is not just a strategic move; it's a human-centric approach that recognizes the dynamic needs of this workforce. Here's an empathetic guide for HR professionals on skill development tailored for gig workers:

a). Understanding Individual Aspirations:

Start by understanding the unique aspirations of gig workers. Engage in open conversations to identify their career goals, skills they wish to develop, and the trajectory they envision. This personalized understanding forms the foundation for effective skills development.

b). Flexible Learning Paths:

Recognize that gig workers often juggle multiple projects and commitments. Design flexible learning paths that allow them to acquire new skills at their own pace. This flexibility not only accommodates their schedules but also demonstrates a commitment to their professional growth.

c). Offering Diverse Learning Formats:

Embrace diverse learning formats that cater to different preferences. Some gig workers might thrive in traditional courses, while others prefer hands-on experiences or mentorship programs. Providing a mix of learning opportunities ensures inclusivity and accessibility.

d). Encouraging Peer-to-Peer Learning:

Facilitate a culture of peer-to-peer learning within the gig workforce. Encourage knowledge-sharing sessions, collaborative projects, and mentorship opportunities. Gig workers often bring a wealth of diverse experiences, and enabling them to learn from each other enhances the overall skill set within the community.

e). Tailoring Development Plans:

Develop individualized development plans based on both the immediate project requirements and the long-term career goals of gig workers. Aligning skills development with their aspirations ensures that the acquired skills contribute to their overall professional journey.

f). Recognizing Soft Skills:

Beyond technical skills, place a spotlight on soft skills development. Effective communication, adaptability, and problem-solving are critical in the gig landscape. Recognize and support the enhancement of these soft skills, as they contribute significantly to a gig worker's success.

g). Utilizing Microlearning Modules:

Embrace microlearning as a powerful tool in the skills development arsenal. Bite-sized modules are well-suited for gig workers who often prefer quick, focused learning sessions that can be seamlessly integrated into their busy schedules.

h). Providing Access to Learning Resources:

Ensure accessibility to a variety of learning resources. Whether it's online courses, webinars, or industry publications, providing gig workers with a curated set of resources empowers them to take control of their learning journey.

i). Recognizing and Celebrating Milestones:

Celebrate milestones in skills development. Whether it's completing a certification, mastering a new technology, or achieving a personal learning goal, recognizing these achievements reinforces the value placed on continuous learning within the gig workforce.

j). Feedback for Continuous Improvement:

Establish a feedback loop for the skills development process. Regularly check in with gig workers to understand their learning experiences, challenges faced, and areas for improvement. This feedback-driven approach ensures that the skills development strategy remains agile and responsive to evolving needs.

In the world of gig work, empowering individuals through skills development is not just about filling gaps; it's about nurturing their professional growth. By understanding their aspirations, providing flexible learning opportunities, and recognizing the importance of both technical and soft skills, HR professionals can create an environment where gig workers thrive, contribute meaningfully, and continuously evolve in their careers.

Balancing Flexibility and Stability: HR's Talent Management Dilemma

Navigating the delicate balance between flexibility and stability in talent management poses a constant dilemma for HR professionals. It's a dance between meeting the dynamic needs of a modern workforce and ensuring the resilience and continuity of the organization. Here's a human perspective on how HR can tackle this intricate challenge:

a). Understanding the Dual Nature:

Acknowledge that the workforce today craves both flexibility and stability. While gig workers and freelancers seek project-based flexibility, full-time employees value the stability that comes with a consistent role and long-term commitment. Striking the right balance involves recognizing and respecting these dual needs.

b). Customizing Work Arrangements:

Embrace the power of customization in work arrangements. Offer flexible schedules, remote work options, and project-based roles for those seeking flexibility. Simultaneously, provide stability through well-defined career paths, mentorship programs, and opportunities for long-term growth for full-time employees.

c). Open Communication Channels:

Foster open communication channels to understand the varied preferences of your workforce. Regularly solicit feedback on work arrangements, assess the needs of different teams, and create an environment where employees feel comfortable expressing their desires for flexibility or stability.

d). Adaptable Talent Management Strategies:

Recognize that talent management strategies need to be as adaptable as the workforce itself. Traditional approaches may not resonate with a workforce that values fluidity. Be ready to tweak strategies, adopting an agile mindset that accommodates the evolving needs of both flexible and stable roles.

e). Offering Skill Development for Adaptability:

Equip your workforce with the skills needed for adaptability. Provide training programs that enhance not only technical competencies but also soft skills like resilience, problem-solving, and adaptability. An adaptable workforce is better prepared to navigate the fine line between flexibility and stability.

f). Building a Culture of Inclusivity:

Foster a culture that values both flexibility and stability. Ensure that the organization's mission and values resonate with all employees, regardless of their work arrangement. A culture of inclusivity minimizes the divide between flexible and stable roles, fostering unity and shared goals.

g). Strategic Succession Planning:

Succession planning is a cornerstone in balancing stability. Identify key roles that require long-term commitment and develop strategic plans for succession. Simultaneously, assess the gig workforce for potential leaders and contributors, ensuring a talent pipeline that's both flexible and stable.

h). Emphasizing Well-being Initiatives:

Acknowledge that the demands of flexibility can sometimes lead to burnout. Prioritize well-being initiatives that support the mental health and work-life balance of both flexible and stable employees. A workforce that feels cared for is more likely to contribute to the organization's long-term success.

i). Building Trust Through Transparency:

Foster trust by being transparent about the organization's vision and future plans. Share insights into how flexibility and stability are integral parts of the overall strategy. When employees understand the organization's direction, they are more likely to align their expectations with its goals.

j). Celebrating Diversity in Work Arrangements:

Celebrate the diversity of work arrangements within the organization. Showcase success stories from both flexible and stable roles. By celebrating diversity, HR can instill a sense of pride and belonging among employees, regardless of their chosen work arrangement.

In essence, balancing flexibility and stability is about recognizing the varied needs of the workforce and crafting talent management strategies that honor those differences. By fostering a culture of adaptability, promoting open communication, and aligning skill development with evolving needs, HR professionals can successfully navigate this delicate dance, ensuring both the agility and resilience of the organization.

4. BEYOND 9 TO 5: ADAPTING HR PRACTICES TO THE GIG ECONOMY

Step into the realm where the clock's hands don't dictate the rhythm of work, and the conventional 9 to 5 is a mere echo of the past. The gig economy beckons, and for HR professionals, it's not just a shift; it's a symphony of adaptability. Beyond the confines of traditional work hours, we find a landscape where flexibility, diversity, and innovation reign supreme. Welcome to the era where HR practices venture "Beyond 9 to 5," shaping a dynamic workplace where gig workers take the stage. It's not just about adapting; it's about orchestrating a future where work knows no bounds. Let's explore the horizons together!

Flexible Work Policies: Crafting a Framework for Success

Crafting a framework for flexible work policies isn't just about adjusting schedules; it's about fostering an environment where individuals can thrive both professionally and personally. Let's delve into the human side of creating a successful framework for flexible work policies:

a). Understanding Individual Needs:

The cornerstone of any successful flexible work policy lies in understanding the unique needs of individuals. Initiate conversations to comprehend their preferences, constraints, and aspirations. Recognizing that one size doesn't fit all sets the stage for a truly inclusive framework.

b). Tailoring Schedules to Foster Productivity:

Flexibility isn't synonymous with chaos. Tailor flexible schedules to enhance productivity. Whether it's compressed workweeks, staggered hours, or remote work options, the goal is to create an environment where individuals can deliver their best work while accommodating their personal circumstances.

c). Communication as the Bedrock:

Clear communication is the bedrock of any flexible work policy. Establish transparent channels for communicating expectations, deadlines, and availability. The more everyone is on the same page, the smoother the transition to flexible work arrangements.

d). Building Trust Through Accountability:

Trust is a two-way street. Foster a culture of accountability where individuals are trusted to manage their responsibilities effectively. Conversely, encourage open communication when challenges arise. A culture of trust forms the foundation of a successful flexible work framework.

e). Providing Technological Support:

Seamless technology is the backbone of flexible work policies. Ensure that individuals have access to the tools and resources they need for effective remote collaboration. Invest in user-friendly platforms that facilitate communication, project management, and virtual collaboration.

f). Encouraging Breaks and Boundaries:

Flexibility should never translate into a 24/7 work mentality. Encourage individuals to establish clear boundaries between work and personal life. Taking breaks, setting realistic expectations, and prioritizing well-being are crucial aspects of a sustainable flexible work framework.

g). Flexibility in Career Development:

Extend flexibility to career development. Provide opportunities for skill development, mentorship, and career growth that can be pursued on individual timelines. A flexible career development approach ensures that individuals can chart their own professional journeys.

h). Regular Check-Ins for Connection:

Flexible work shouldn't mean isolation. Schedule regular check-ins to maintain a sense of connection among team members. Virtual coffee chats, team meetings, and informal catch-ups foster a collaborative environment even in the virtual landscape.

i). Addressing Potential Bias:

Be mindful of potential bias in flexible work arrangements. Ensure that opportunities for projects, promotions, and recognition are equally accessible to individuals regardless of their work structure. Addressing bias reinforces the fairness of the flexible work framework.

j). Evaluating and Iterating:

Flexibility is an evolving concept. Regularly evaluate the effectiveness of the flexible work policies. Solicit feedback, analyze outcomes, and be open to iterating the framework based on the evolving needs and dynamics of the workforce.

In essence, crafting a successful framework for flexible work policies is about putting people first. By understanding their needs, fostering a culture of trust, and continuously adapting to create a harmonious blend of flexibility and productivity, organizations can cultivate an environment where individuals can truly thrive.

The Evolution of Work: HR's Role in Redefining Job Structures

The evolution of work is not just a shift in routine; it's a profound transformation that demands HR to play a central role in redefining job structures. Let's explore the human side of this evolution and the pivotal role HR professionals play in shaping the future of work:

a). Embracing Fluidity in Roles:

Gone are the days of rigid job descriptions. HR must embrace the fluidity of roles in the evolving work landscape. Recognize that employees bring a spectrum of skills and talents that can be harnessed in dynamic ways. Encourage a culture where individuals can explore and contribute beyond predefined boundaries.

b). Fostering a Culture of Continuous Learning:

The evolution of work is synonymous with continuous learning. HR should champion a culture that values upskilling, reskilling, and embracing new competencies. Encourage employees to be perpetual learners, ensuring they stay relevant in a landscape of ever-changing job requirements.

c). Adapting to Remote and Hybrid Models:

The traditional notion of a 9-to-5 office job is evolving. HR must adapt to remote and hybrid work models. This involves creating policies that support flexible work arrangements, leveraging technology for seamless collaboration, and prioritizing employee well-being in diverse work environments.

d). Facilitating Cross-Functional Collaboration:

Silos are crumbling as collaboration becomes a linchpin of success. HR professionals should facilitate cross-functional collaboration, breaking down departmental barriers. Encourage employees to collaborate on diverse projects, fostering a culture where varied skill sets converge for innovative outcomes.

e). Shifting Focus to Outcomes, Not Hours:

The focus should shift from counting hours to measuring outcomes. HR's role is to redefine success metrics, emphasizing the impact of an employee's contributions rather than the time spent on a task. This shift aligns with the evolving understanding that productivity is not confined to a specific time frame.

f). Creating Agile Job Structures:

Job structures should mirror the agility of the modern workforce. HR must work towards creating agile job structures that can adapt to the ebbs and flows of business demands. This involves reevaluating job roles regularly and ensuring they align with the strategic goals of the organization.

g). Emphasizing Employee Well-being:

As work evolves, so does the emphasis on employee well-being. HR should take a proactive approach to address the physical and mental health of employees. Implement well-being programs, encourage breaks, and create an environment that prioritizes a healthy work-life balance.

h). Promoting Diversity and Inclusion:

The evolving workplace thrives on diverse perspectives. HR plays key important roles in promoting diversity and inclusion. Actively seek diverse talent, ensure equitable opportunities, and foster an inclusive environment where every individual feels valued and heard.

i). Navigating the Gig Economy:

The gig economy is an integral part of the evolving work landscape. HR professionals need to navigate this terrain by adapting recruitment strategies, fostering a sense of community among gig workers, and recognizing the unique contributions they bring to the organization.

j). Communicating Transparently:

Transparent communication is the glue that binds the evolving workplace together. HR should communicate openly about organizational changes, evolving job structures, and future plans. This transparency builds trust and ensures that employees are informed and engaged in the journey of transformation.

In essence, the evolution of work requires HR professionals to be architects of change, shaping job structures that align with the dynamic needs of the workforce. By fostering a culture of continuous learning, embracing agility, and prioritizing the well-being and diversity of employees, HR becomes a catalyst in redefining how we approach work in the modern era.

Remote Collaboration: Tools and Techniques for HR Professionals

Navigating the realm of remote collaboration as an HR professional involves more than just mastering technology; it's about fostering genuine connections in a virtual landscape. Let's explore the human side of remote collaboration and delve into the tools and techniques that can elevate HR's role in this digital age:

a). Video Conferencing with a Personal Touch:

While video conferencing tools are ubiquitous, HR can add a personal touch. Encourage the use of video during virtual meetings to foster a sense of connection. Seeing faces and expressions helps build relationships, making remote collaboration more human and engaging.

b). Interactive Collaboration Platforms:

Beyond emails, embrace interactive collaboration platforms. Tools like Slack, Microsoft Teams, or Asana facilitate real-time communication, file sharing, and project collaboration. Create channels for different teams or projects to streamline communication and enhance teamwork.

c). Virtual Coffee Chats and Team Building:

Remote work shouldn't mean the end of coffee chats and team building. Schedule virtual coffee breaks or casual team-building activities. Platforms like Zoom or Google Meet can be used for informal gatherings, allowing team members to connect on a personal level.

d). Employee Recognition Platforms:

Recognition is vital in remote settings. Utilize employee recognition platforms like Bonusly or Kudos to celebrate achievements publicly. Acknowledging hard work and achievements fosters a positive virtual work environment.

e). Digital Whiteboarding for Brainstorming:

Recreate the magic of in-person brainstorming with digital whiteboarding tools. Miro or MURAL allow teams to collaborate visually in real-time. These tools are excellent for brainstorming sessions, project planning, and fostering creativity.

f). Surveys for Employee Feedback:

Keep a finger on the pulse of your remote workforce through regular surveys. Tools like SurveyMonkey or Google Forms allow HR to gather feedback on employee well-being, remote work challenges, and suggestions for improvement.

g). Webinars for Learning and Development:

Leverage webinars for ongoing learning and development initiatives. Platforms like Zoom Webinars or Microsoft Teams Live Events enable HR to host virtual training sessions, workshops, or guest speaker events to enrich the professional growth of remote teams.

i). Well-being Apps for Employee Support:

Employee well-being is paramount in remote settings. Introduce well-being apps like Headspace or Calm to support mental health. Encourage employees to take advantage of resources that promote relaxation, mindfulness, and stress reduction.

j); Cloud-Based HR Management Systems:

Move HR processes to the cloud with platforms like Workday or BambooHR. Cloud-based HR systems streamline tasks like performance management, benefits administration, and employee records, providing accessibility to the entire remote workforce.

k). Open Communication Channels:

The foundation of successful remote collaboration is open communication. Emphasize transparent communication channels, whether through regular town hall meetings, team updates, or dedicated communication platforms. The more information flows freely, the stronger the virtual connections become.

In the realm of remote collaboration, HR professionals become architects of connectivity. By infusing technology with a human touch, utilizing interactive platforms, and prioritizing employee well-being, HR can not only bridge the physical gaps but also create a virtual workspace where remote teams feel connected, valued, and part of a unified mission.

Measuring Success: Key Performance Indicators for Gig Employee Productivity

Measuring the success of gig employee productivity goes beyond the conventional metrics; it's about capturing the essence of their contributions in a dynamic work landscape. Here's a human-centric take on key performance indicators (KPIs) that resonate with the unique nature of gig work:

a). Project Delivery Timeframes:

In the gig realm, time is often of the essence. Measure the time gig employees take to deliver projects. A prompt turnaround indicates efficiency, adaptability, and a commitment to meeting deadlines.

b). *Quality of Deliverables:*

It's not just about completing tasks; it's about the quality of the deliverables. Assess the output of gig employees by gauging the excellence and impact of their work. Quality is a powerful indicator of the value they bring to projects.

c). *Client Satisfaction and Feedback:*

The satisfaction of clients or project stakeholders is a tangible measure of success. Collect feedback on the gig employee's performance. Positive reviews not only validate their efforts but also contribute to building a positive reputation within the gig community.

d). *Adaptability to Change:*

Gig workers thrive in dynamic environments. Assess their adaptability to changes in project scopes, timelines, or work processes. The ability to pivot seamlessly is a key indicator of their resilience and versatility.

e). *Feedback from Team Collaboration:*

In a gig setting, collaboration is paramount. Collect feedback from team members on the gig employee's collaborative efforts. Strong teamwork and effective communication contribute significantly to the overall success of a project.

f). Number of Successful Projects Completed:

Keep a tally of the number of successful projects completed by gig employees. This metric provides a holistic view of their track record and showcases their ability to consistently contribute to project success.

g). Communication and Responsiveness:

Effective communication is the backbone of gig work. Evaluate gig employees on their responsiveness to messages, clarity in communication, and their ability to stay connected virtually. Strong communication skills is prerequisite for seamless collaboration.

h). Achievement of Key Milestones:

Break down projects into key milestones and track the gig employee's progress. Achieving milestones on time indicates progress and ensures that the project is on track for successful completion.

i). Utilization of Available Resources:

Assess how gig employees utilize available resources. This includes their ability to leverage technology, access relevant information, and collaborate effectively. Resource optimization reflects their efficiency in navigating the gig landscape.

j). Professional Growth and Skill Development:

Measure the gig employee's commitment to professional growth. Track their participation in training programs, acquisition of new skills, and engagement in opportunities for upskilling. A focus on continuous improvement is indicative of long-term success.

In the realm of gig work, traditional KPIs may not capture the full spectrum of contributions. By considering project-specific elements, collaboration dynamics, and the adaptability of gig employees, organizations can create a comprehensive framework for measuring success that aligns with the unique nature of gig work.

5. THE GIG WORK PARADOX: CHALLENGES AND OPPORTUNITIES FOR HR LEADERS

Welcome to the crossroads where the gig work paradox unfolds—a landscape where challenges and opportunities entwine, presenting a dynamic tableau for HR leaders. In this realm, every hurdle is a stepping stone, and every challenge is an opportunity waiting to be seized. Join us as we navigate the intricate dance of gig work, where HR leaders play a central role in unraveling the paradox. It's not just about addressing challenges; it's about leveraging them as catalysts for innovation and growth. Welcome to "The Gig Work Paradox," where the road less traveled becomes the canvas for HR leaders to paint a narrative of resilience and triumph

Navigating Legal Complexities: Compliance Challenges in Gig Employment

Navigating the legal complexities of gig employment is like charting unexplored territory. It's a landscape filled with nuances that require a human touch to address the compliance challenges effectively. Let's explore the intricacies and challenges through a more personal lens:

a). Defining Employment Status:

The very foundation of compliance in gig employment lies in defining the employment status. It's not just about labels; it's about understanding the nature of the relationship. HR needs to delve into the intricacies to distinguish between independent contractors and employees, as misclassification can lead to legal complications.

b). Crafting Clear Contracts:

Contracts are the backbone of gig employment. Craft contracts with clarity and transparency. Clearly outline the terms of engagement, scope of work, payment structures, and any limitations. A well-defined contract serves as a roadmap, minimizing legal ambiguities.

c). Navigating Multijurisdictional Challenges:

Gig work often transcends geographical boundaries. HR professionals must grapple with the complexities of compliance in multiple jurisdictions. Each region may have its own set of rules and regulations, making it essential to stay informed and adapt practices accordingly.

d). Addressing Wage and Hour Compliance:

Wage and hour compliance is a constant tightrope walk. HR needs to ensure that gig workers are compensated fairly and in adherence to local labor laws. Tracking working hours, implementing overtime policies, and ensuring timely payments are critical components of compliance.

e). Benefits and Entitlements:

Gig workers aren't always entitled to traditional employee benefits, but compliance demands a thorough understanding of applicable laws. HR professionals need to carefully navigate benefit structures, ensuring that gig workers receive fair compensation while staying within legal boundaries.

f). Data Protection and Privacy:

In the digital age, data protection is a paramount concern. HR must establish robust measures to ensure the confidentiality and privacy of both employee and company data. Compliance with data protection laws is not just a legal obligation but a commitment to ethical practices.

g). *Mitigating Discrimination Risks:*

Discrimination risks loom large, especially in remote collaborations. HR needs to actively work toward preventing discrimination, ensuring fair treatment regardless of employment status. Policies and practices should be designed to foster inclusivity and diversity within the gig workforce.

h). *Ensuring Occupational Safety:*

Occupational safety isn't confined to traditional workplaces. HR must extend safety considerations to gig workers. Establish guidelines that prioritize their well-being during tasks and implement safety measures that align with the nature of their work.

i). *Keeping Abreast of Legal Updates:*

The legal landscape is ever-evolving. HR professionals need to be vigilant about staying abreast of legal updates related to gig employment. Regularly review and update policies to align with any changes in local, regional, or national regulations.

j). Cultivating Open Communication:

Perhaps the most human aspect of compliance is open communication. Foster an environment where gig workers feel comfortable expressing concerns or seeking clarification on legal matters. An open dialogue ensures that compliance isn't just a checkbox but a shared commitment to ethical and legal practices.

In navigating the legal complexities of gig employment, HR professionals become interpreters of law, translators of policy, and architects of fair practices. By embracing clarity, transparency, and open communication, HR can humanize the compliance landscape, creating an environment where gig workers feel not just legally protected but valued and respected in their professional engagements.

Building Trust: Overcoming Challenges in Remote Gig Management

Building trust in the realm of remote gig management is akin to nurturing a delicate flower in different climates. It requires careful attention, adaptability, and a human touch. Let's explore the challenges and approaches to fostering trust in this dynamic landscape:

a). Communication Hurdles:

Remote gig management often grapples with communication challenges. Trust is built on a foundation of clear, consistent, and open communication. Overcome hurdles by embracing various communication channels, scheduling regular check-ins, and encouraging an environment where questions and concerns are welcomed.

b). Establishing Clear Expectations:

Ambiguity breeds mistrust. Set clear expectations from the outset. Clearly define project scopes, timelines, and deliverables. When gig workers have a crystal-clear understanding of what's expected, trust naturally follows.

c). Mitigating Isolation and Disconnect:

Remote work can lead to feelings of isolation. Combat this by fostering a sense of connection. Implement virtual team-building activities, encourage casual conversations, and create a supportive community. Trust flourishes when individuals feel they are part of a collective effort.

d). Ensuring Fair Compensation:

Trust and fair compensation go hand in hand. Be transparent about payment structures, rates, and any relevant financial details. Timely and fair compensation builds a sense of reliability and fosters trust between gig workers and management.

e). Providing Adequate Resources:

Lack of resources can erode trust. Ensure that gig workers have access to the tools, information, and support they need. Whether it's technology, training, or project-related resources, providing what's necessary demonstrates commitment and reliability.

f). Addressing Security Concerns:

In the virtual realm, security is paramount. Address concerns related to data security and confidentiality. Implement robust security measures, communicate them clearly, and assure gig workers that their work and information are handled with the utmost care.

g). Building a Supportive Culture:

Trust flourishes in a culture of support. Encourage a culture where gig workers feel valued, appreciated, and supported. Recognize their contributions publicly, offer guidance when needed, and create an environment that prioritizes collective success.

h). Flexibility in Work Arrangements:

Trust is nurtured through flexibility. Acknowledge the unique needs and preferences of gig workers when it comes to work arrangements. Providing flexibility in schedules or project structures demonstrates a commitment to accommodating individual circumstances.

i). *Prompt Issue Resolution:*

Address issues promptly and transparently. When challenges arise, deal with them openly, communicate solutions clearly, and ensure that gig workers feel heard. Swift and effective issue resolution builds confidence in the management's commitment to a positive working relationship.

j). *Cultivating Personal Connections:*

Trust is not only about work; it's also about personal connections. Take the time to know gig workers as individuals. Learn about their interests, acknowledge milestones, and show genuine interest in their well-being. Personal connections foster a deeper level of trust.

In the world of remote gig management, trust is the glue that binds relationships. By proactively addressing communication hurdles, establishing clear expectations, and fostering a supportive culture, HR professionals can create an environment where trust thrives naturally, ensuring a successful and collaborative partnership with gig workers.

Balancing Autonomy and Accountability: HR's Conundrum

Balancing autonomy and accountability in the workplace is a nuanced dance that HR professionals often find themselves orchestrating. It's a conundrum where fostering independence meets the need for responsibility. Let's explore the human side of this delicate equilibrium:

a). Empowering Autonomy:

Autonomy isn't just a buzzword; it's about empowering individuals to take ownership of their work. HR plays a crucial role in creating an environment where employees feel trusted to make decisions, explore creative solutions, and drive their own projects.

b). Defining Clear Expectations:

Autonomy flourishes when it walks hand in hand with clarity. HR needs to set clear expectations regarding goals, objectives, and performance standards. Providing a roadmap ensures that autonomy isn't a leap into the unknown but a guided journey.

c). Encouraging Informed Decision-Making:

Autonomy doesn't mean isolation. HR should foster a culture where informed decision-making is encouraged. Provide access to information, resources, and mentorship. When employees are equipped with knowledge, their autonomy is grounded in a solid foundation.

e). Open Communication Channels:

The bridge between autonomy and accountability is built on open communication. HR professionals need to establish channels where employees feel comfortable seeking guidance, sharing challenges, and discussing their decisions. A culture of open communication ensures that autonomy doesn't lead to silos.

f). Celebrating Individual Contributions:

Autonomy shines when individual contributions are celebrated. HR should actively recognize and appreciate the unique contributions of employees. Whether it's through public acknowledgment or team celebrations, highlighting individual efforts reinforces the value of autonomy.

g). Measuring Impact, Not Just Activity:

In the quest for accountability, HR needs to shift the focus from mere activity to impact. Instead of micromanaging tasks, measure the broader impact of employees' contributions. This approach ensures that accountability is tied to meaningful outcomes rather than a checklist of activities.

h). Providing Feedback for Growth:

Accountability and growth go hand in hand. HR professionals should provide constructive feedback that promotes continuous improvement. Feedback sessions should be framed not as critiques but as opportunities for development, aligning accountability with personal and professional growth.

i). Creating a Culture of Trust:

Trust is the bedrock of balancing autonomy and accountability. HR must cultivate a culture where trust permeates every interaction. When employees trust that their autonomy is respected and that they are held accountable for meaningful contributions, a healthy equilibrium is achieved.

j). Tailoring Management Styles:

Recognize that different individuals thrive with different levels of autonomy. HR should tailor management styles to accommodate varied preferences. Some employees may flourish with more independence, while others may prefer a more guided approach. Flexibility in management styles ensures inclusivity.

k). Aligning Autonomy with Organizational Values:

The delicate balance lies in aligning autonomy with organizational values. HR should ensure that the exercise of autonomy doesn't compromise ethical standards or the overall mission of the company. When autonomy is in harmony with core values, accountability becomes a shared commitment.

In the intricate dance between autonomy and accountability, HR professionals emerge as choreographers, orchestrating a symphony that harmonizes individual empowerment with collective responsibility. By fostering open communication, celebrating contributions, and tailoring approaches to individual needs, HR transforms the conundrum into a well-balanced and dynamic workplace ecosystem.

HR's Role in Mitigating Risks: A Comprehensive Approach to Gig Work

Navigating the landscape of gig work introduces a myriad of risks, and HR's role becomes pivotal in mitigating these challenges. It's a multifaceted journey that goes beyond policies and procedures; it's about embracing a comprehensive approach that puts the well-being of both the organization and gig workers at the forefront.

a). Strategic Onboarding and Orientation:

Mitigating risks starts with a solid foundation – strategic onboarding. HR should design comprehensive onboarding processes that not only acquaint gig workers with their roles but also educate them on the company's values, policies, and expectations. Setting the right tone from the beginning minimizes potential pitfalls.

b). Clear Communication of Expectations:

Risk mitigation thrives on clear communication. HR professionals should articulate expectations transparently. From project deliverables to timelines, ensuring that gig workers have a crystal-clear understanding helps prevent misunderstandings that could lead to risks.

c). Dynamic Risk Assessments:

Risks in the gig landscape are ever-evolving. HR should adopt a dynamic approach to risk assessments. Regularly evaluate potential risks associated with gig work, considering factors such as project complexity, data sensitivity, and external market influences.

d). Compliance and Legal Adherence:

The legal intricacies of gig work demand HR's vigilance. Stay abreast of local, regional, and national regulations governing gig employment. Ensure that contracts, payment structures, and work arrangements align with legal standards to mitigate compliance risks.

e). Data Security Measures:

In the digital age, data security is paramount. HR professionals must implement robust measures to safeguard sensitive information handled by gig workers. This involves not only providing secure platforms but also educating gig workers on best practices for data protection.

f). Insurance and Liability Considerations:

Assessing and addressing insurance and liability aspects is a crucial component of risk mitigation. HR should work alongside legal experts to ensure that gig workers and the organization are adequately covered in case of unforeseen incidents or disputes.

g). Continuous Performance Monitoring:

Proactive risk mitigation involves continuous performance monitoring. Establish metrics to measure the performance of gig workers, ensuring that deviations from expectations are identified early. Regular check-ins and performance reviews contribute to risk mitigation by addressing issues promptly.

h). Building Resilience in Talent Pipelines:

HR's role extends beyond individual projects. Mitigating risks includes building resilience in talent pipelines. Diversify the pool of gig workers, cultivate long-term relationships, and create contingency plans to address sudden changes or disruptions in the gig workforce.

i). Investing in Cybersecurity Training:

Cybersecurity risks are a prevalent concern in remote gig collaborations. HR should invest in cybersecurity training for gig workers, educating them on potential threats and best practices for maintaining a secure digital environment. Awareness is a powerful tool in risk mitigation.

j). Proactive Conflict Resolution Strategies:

Conflicts can arise in any work setting, and gig work is no exception. HR professionals should proactively develop conflict resolution strategies. Establish clear channels for dispute resolution, encourage open communication, and provide mediation resources to address conflicts swiftly.

In the realm of gig work, HR becomes the guardian of a comprehensive risk mitigation strategy. By focusing on clear communication, compliance, data security, and proactive measures to address evolving challenges, HR professionals can create an environment where risks are not just managed but transformed into opportunities for growth and resilience.

6. FREELANCERS AND FLEXIBILITY: CRAFTING HR POLICIES FOR THE GIG WORKFORCE

Welcome to the era of freelancers and flexibility, where the traditional notions of employment dissolve, and a vibrant gig workforce takes center stage. Crafting HR policies in this dynamic landscape is not just a task; it's an art of balancing structure and adaptability. Join us as we delve into the world where freelancers thrive and flexibility reigns supreme. In this journey, HR policies become more than guidelines; they become the architects of a workplace that embraces the diverse talents and work styles of the gig workforce. Welcome to the realm of "Freelancers and Flexibility," where HR policies shape a canvas that celebrates the essence of the gig economy.

Policy Frameworks for Remote Gig Workers: A Practical Guide

Crafting policy frameworks for remote gig workers requires a blend of practicality, empathy, and foresight. It's about creating guidelines that not only protect the interests of the organization but also foster a supportive and equitable environment for gig workers. Let's explore this process with a human touch:

a). Flexible Work Arrangements:

Embrace flexibility as the cornerstone of your policy framework. Recognize that gig workers value autonomy in their work. Craft policies that allow for flexible schedules, remote work options, and project-based arrangements, acknowledging the unique needs of the gig workforce.

b). Clear Communication Protocols:

Communication is the lifeblood of remote gig work. Establish clear protocols for communication channels, response times, and expectations. Transparent communication not only fosters collaboration but also helps in mitigating potential misunderstandings.

c). *Project Scope and Deliverables:*

Define project scopes and deliverables comprehensively. Clearly outline the expectations for each project, including timelines, milestones, and key performance indicators. This clarity not only guides gig workers but also ensures alignment with organizational objectives.

d). *Payment and Compensation Structures:*

Transparent payment structures are essential for building trust. Clearly articulate how gig workers will be compensated, including rates, payment schedules, and any additional incentives. Clarity in compensation helps in avoiding disputes and building a positive working relationship.

e). *Data Security and Confidentiality:*

Address the crucial aspect of data security. Clearly communicate the organization's commitment to protecting sensitive information. Provide guidelines on secure data handling, use of company resources, and adherence to confidentiality standards to mitigate risks.

f). *Performance Metrics and Reviews:*

Develop fair and objective performance metrics. Outline how gig worker performance will be evaluated, including regular reviews. Constructive feedback and performance assessments contribute not only to growth but also to a sense of accountability.

g). *Professional Development Opportunities:*

Demonstrate a commitment to the professional growth of gig workers. Integrate opportunities for skill development, training programs, and mentorship into the policy framework. This not only enhances the skills of gig workers but also showcases the organization's investment in their long-term success.

h). *Inclusivity and Diversity Initiatives:*

Inclusivity is integral to a thriving gig ecosystem. Implement policies that promote diversity and equal opportunities. Foster an environment where gig workers from various backgrounds feel included and valued, contributing to a more enriching collaborative experience.

i). *Conflict Resolution Mechanisms:*

Address conflicts proactively by establishing clear conflict resolution mechanisms. Provide guidelines on how disputes will be handled, ensuring a fair and impartial process. Open communication channels for conflict resolution contribute to a positive work environment.

j). Regular Policy Reviews and Updates:

Recognize that the gig landscape is dynamic. Regularly review and update policies to adapt to evolving needs, market trends, and regulatory changes. A flexible policy framework ensures that the organization remains agile in responding to the challenges of the gig economy.

In the realm of remote gig work, policy frameworks should be more than rules on paper; they should be guiding principles that create a conducive and supportive environment. By infusing policies with flexibility, transparency, and a genuine commitment to the well-being and professional growth of gig workers, organizations can foster a mutually beneficial relationship that goes beyond transactional engagements.

Health and Benefits: Adapting Packages for Freelance Talent

Tailoring health and benefits packages for freelance talent involves a delicate dance of addressing individual needs while aligning with organizational values. It's about recognizing the unique challenges freelancers face and offering support that goes beyond the traditional employment model. Let's dive into the human side of adapting health and benefits packages for freelance talent:

a). Comprehensive Health Coverage Options:

Extend a helping hand by offering freelancers access to comprehensive health coverage. This could involve partnering with health insurance providers or exploring options for group coverage. Providing a safety net for health-related concerns demonstrates a genuine commitment to the well-being of freelance talent.

b). Flexible Wellness Programs:

Wellness isn't a one-size-fits-all concept. Craft wellness programs that are adaptable to the diverse needs of freelancers. This might include virtual fitness classes, mental health resources, or wellness stipends that allow freelancers to invest in activities that contribute to their overall well-being.

c). Financial Well-being Support:

Recognize the financial ebbs and flows that freelancers often face. Consider offering financial well-being resources, such as workshops on budgeting, access to financial advisors, or tools that help freelancers manage their income and plan for the future.

d). Customizable Benefit Packages:

Embrace the diversity of freelance talent by providing customizable benefit packages. Allow freelancers to tailor their benefits to align with their individual preferences and needs. This flexibility not only accommodates varied lifestyles but also fosters a sense of autonomy.

e). Access to Professional Development:

Elevate your support beyond traditional benefits. Offer freelancers access to professional development opportunities. This might include online courses, workshops, or mentorship programs that contribute to their skill enhancement and career growth.

f). Remote Work Support:

Freelancers often work in decentralized environments. Provide resources to support their remote work setup. This could involve stipends for home office equipment, virtual collaboration tools, or even coworking space memberships to enhance their work environment.

g). Family-Friendly Benefits:

Acknowledge that freelancers have families and personal commitments. Consider family-friendly benefits such as parental leave, childcare support, or resources that assist freelancers in balancing their professional and personal lives.

h). Clear Communication on Benefits:

Communication is key. Clearly articulate the benefits available to freelancers. Provide easily accessible information on how to enroll, access resources, and make the most of the offered benefits. Transparent communication builds trust and ensures freelancers feel supported.

i). Community Building Initiatives:

Freelancers may miss out on the camaraderie of a traditional office. Facilitate community building initiatives that connect freelancers with each other and the broader organizational culture. This might involve virtual meetups, networking events, or online forums where freelancers can share experiences and insights.

j). Regular Check-Ins and Feedback:

Establish a feedback loop. Regularly check in with freelancers to understand their needs, gather insights on the effectiveness of the benefits offered, and provide a platform for them to express any concerns. This ongoing dialogue reinforces the organization's commitment to their well-being.

In the evolving landscape of work, adapting health and benefits packages for freelance talent is not just a policy; it's a demonstration of a company's commitment to the holistic well-being of its extended workforce. By tailoring packages with empathy, flexibility, and a keen understanding of freelance dynamics, organizations can create an environment where freelancers not only contribute their best work but feel genuinely cared for and valued.

Fair Compensation: Strategies for Setting Rates in the Gig Economy

Determining fair compensation in the gig economy is a nuanced challenge that requires a delicate balance between recognizing the value of individual contributions and aligning with market standards. Let's explore the human side of setting rates in the gig economy and strategies that ensure fairness for both parties involved:

a). *Understanding the Value Exchange:*

Compensation isn't just about numbers; it's a reflection of the value exchange between the gig worker and the client. Encourage open conversations to understand the scope of work, the unique skills brought to the table, and the impact the gig will have on the client's objectives.

b). Transparent Communication on Rates:

Transparency builds trust. Clearly communicate the rates and payment structures upfront. Provide a breakdown of how rates are determined, whether it's based on hours worked, project milestones, or the complexity of the task. This transparency sets the stage for a collaborative and trusting relationship.

c). Researching Market Standards:

Stay informed about market standards in your industry. Research what other gig workers with similar skills and experience are charging. This benchmarking ensures that rates are competitive and reflective of the current market landscape.

d). Customizing Rates Based on Expertise:

Recognize that not all gig workers are created equal in terms of expertise. Tailor rates based on the level of skill, experience, and specialization brought to the gig. This acknowledges and values the unique strengths each gig worker contributes.

e). Flexible Pricing Models:

Embrace flexibility in pricing models. Some gigs may benefit from hourly rates, while others might be better suited for project-based or retainer arrangements. Having a variety of pricing models allows for customization based on the nature of the work and the preferences of both parties.

f). Considering Overhead and Expenses:

Gig workers often bear their own overhead costs. Factor in expenses such as equipment, software, and self-employment taxes when setting rates. Acknowledging and compensating for these additional costs ensures that gig workers are not undervalued.

g). Negotiating Fairly and Respectfully:

Negotiation is inherent in the gig economy. Approach negotiations with fairness and respect. Understand the needs and constraints on both sides, and work towards a mutually beneficial agreement. A respectful negotiation process lays the groundwork for a positive working relationship.

h). Providing Performance Incentives:

Consider incorporating performance incentives into compensation structures. If a gig worker exceeds expectations or achieves specific milestones, offering bonuses or performance-based rewards reinforces the principle of fair compensation tied to tangible contributions.

i). Regularly Reviewing Compensation Structures:

The gig economy is dynamic. Regularly review and update compensation structures to stay responsive to changes in market conditions, industry trends, and the evolving skillsets of gig workers. This adaptability ensures that compensation remains fair and competitive.

j). Seeking Feedback on Compensation:

Actively seek feedback from gig workers on compensation structures. Understand their perspectives, challenges, and expectations. This feedback loop not only demonstrates a commitment to fairness but also provides valuable insights for refining compensation strategies.

In the human-centered approach to setting rates in the gig economy, fairness isn't just a matter of numbers; it's a commitment to recognizing and valuing the contributions of each individual. By fostering open communication, flexibility, and a continual feedback loop, organizations can create an environment where fair compensation becomes an integral part of a positive and collaborative gig work experience.

Building a Supportive Ecosystem: HR's Role in Freelancer Well-being

Creating a supportive ecosystem for freelancers is not just about transactions; it's about recognizing the humanity in the gig economy and fostering an environment where freelancers feel valued and cared for. Here's a glimpse into HR's role in building this supportive ecosystem for freelancer well-being:

a). Open Lines of Communication:

HR serves as the bridge between the organization and freelancers. Establish open lines of communication, creating a space where freelancers feel comfortable sharing their concerns, asking questions, and expressing their needs. Transparent communication forms the foundation of a supportive relationship.

b). Understanding Individual Needs:

Every freelancer is unique, with distinct needs and preferences. HR professionals play a crucial role in understanding these individual nuances. Through conversations, surveys, or regular check-ins, gain insights into what freelancers value, how they prefer to work, and what support mechanisms would enhance their well-being.

c). Providing Access to Resources:

Empower freelancers by providing access to resources that contribute to their well-being. This could include wellness programs, mental health resources, or even educational materials. By extending support beyond the confines of work, HR becomes a facilitator of holistic well-being.

d). Flexible Work Arrangements:

Recognize the flexibility that freelancers cherish. HR should actively advocate for and implement policies that allow freelancers to manage their work in a way that aligns with their personal and professional lives. Flexibility contributes to a healthier work-life balance.

e). Timely and Fair Compensation:

The timely and fair compensation of freelancers is a cornerstone of well-being. HR professionals should streamline payment processes, provide clarity on compensation structures, and ensure that freelancers feel valued for their contributions. Fair compensation is a tangible expression of respect.

f). Building a Sense of Community:

Freelancers can sometimes feel isolated. HR's role involves creating a sense of community. This could include virtual meetups, networking events, or even online forums where freelancers can connect, share experiences, and feel part of a larger professional family.

g). Recognition and Appreciation:

Acknowledge the contributions of freelancers. Regularly recognize and appreciate their efforts, whether through public acknowledgments, awards, or simple expressions of gratitude. Feeling valued fosters a positive relationship and contributes to overall well-being.

h). Providing Professional Development Opportunities:

Support the growth of freelancers by offering professional development opportunities. This could involve access to training programs, mentorship initiatives, or avenues for skill enhancement. Investing in their professional journey demonstrates a commitment to their long-term success.

i). Creating a Safe and Inclusive Environment:

Freelancers should feel safe and included in the organizational culture. HR plays a vital role in fostering an environment free from discrimination, where diversity is celebrated, and freelancers feel that their contributions are genuinely welcomed and respected.

j). Regular Check-Ins for Feedback:

Actively seek feedback from freelancers. Regular check-ins provide an opportunity for them to share their experiences, voice concerns, and contribute to the continuous improvement of the supportive ecosystem. Feedback loops are a powerful tool in enhancing well-being.

In the evolving landscape of work, HR's role in building a supportive ecosystem for freelancer well-being transcends traditional boundaries. By prioritizing open communication, understanding individual needs, and fostering a culture of recognition and inclusivity, HR professionals become architects of a gig economy where freelancers not only thrive professionally but also experience a genuine sense of well-being and belonging.

7. AGILE HR IN THE GIG ERA: MAXIMIZING PERFORMANCE IN A CHANGING LANDSCAPE

In the ever-evolving landscape of the gig economy, agility is not just a strategy; it's a necessity. HR professionals find themselves at the forefront, navigating the twists and turns of a dynamic work environment. "Agile HR in the Gig Era" isn't just a guide; it's a playbook for maximizing performance amidst the ever-changing rhythms of the gig landscape. Join us as we uncover the strategies that redefine HR in an era where adaptability isn't a choice; it's a core competency. Buckle up as we explore the art of agility in HR and unlock the potential for peak performance in the gig economy

Agile Methodologies: Applying Scrum to HR Practices

Applying Scrum, an agile methodology, to HR practices is like injecting a dose of dynamism into the traditional realms of Human Resources. It's not just about managing projects; it's about fostering adaptability, collaboration, and a human-centric approach to HR. Let's delve into how Scrum can infuse agility into HR processes:

a). Sprints in Recruitment:

Think of recruitment as a series of sprints. Break down the hiring process into manageable chunks, setting short-term goals and milestones. This agile approach allows HR to adapt quickly to changing talent needs, ensuring a more responsive and efficient recruitment process.

b). Daily Stand-ups for Team Alignment:

Adopt the daily stand-up ritual for team alignment. Regular, brief check-ins keep HR teams on the same page, fostering collaboration and transparency. It's a chance to share updates, address challenges, and ensure everyone is moving in sync towards HR goals.

c). Backlog Management for HR Tasks:

Treat HR tasks as items in a backlog. Prioritize them based on urgency and impact. This ensures that HR teams are always focusing on the most valuable and strategic tasks, providing a structured approach to managing the myriad responsibilities within HR.

d).Scrum Master for Process Facilitation:

Appoint an HR Scrum Master to facilitate processes. This role involves removing impediments, ensuring that HR teams have the resources they need, and fostering a culture of continuous improvement. The Scrum Master is the guardian of agility within HR practices.

e). Retrospectives for Continuous Improvement:

After HR initiatives or projects, conduct retrospectives. Reflect on what worked well, identify areas for improvement, and implement changes in the next iteration. This iterative feedback loop ensures that HR processes evolve and become more effective over time.

f). User Stories for Employee Experience:

Craft user stories to enhance the employee experience. Understand the needs and expectations of employees, and design HR processes that align with their journey. This user-centric approach ensures that HR initiatives resonate with and cater to the diverse needs of the workforce.

g). Cross-Functional HR Teams:

Embrace cross-functional HR teams. Instead of siloed departments, form teams that bring together diverse HR skills. This structure enhances collaboration, breaks down departmental barriers, and allows for a more holistic approach to HR challenges.

h). Kanban Boards for Visual Management:

Visualize HR workflows using Kanban boards. This provides a clear, real-time overview of ongoing tasks, their status, and potential bottlenecks. Visual management enhances transparency and allows HR teams to respond swiftly to emerging needs.

i). Scrum Events for HR Planning:

Integrate Scrum events into HR planning. Conduct sprint planning sessions, review progress in sprint reviews, and adapt plans in sprint retrospectives. This rhythmic cadence ensures that HR remains agile in responding to changing organizational dynamics.

j). Agile Mindset in HR Culture:

Cultivate an agile mindset within the HR culture. Encourage adaptability, collaboration, and a willingness to embrace change. This cultural shift is the foundation for successfully applying Scrum principles to HR practices.

In weaving Scrum into HR practices, it's not just about adopting a methodology; it's about fostering a cultural shift that values agility, collaboration, and continuous improvement. By applying Scrum principles, HR becomes not just a support function but an integral part of organizational agility, ensuring that human resources evolve in sync with the ever-changing dynamics of the workplace.

Real-Time Feedback: Enhancing Performance Management in Gig Teams

In the dynamic realm of gig teams, real-time feedback is like a compass guiding performance, fostering growth, and building a collaborative ethos. Let's delve into how injecting real-time feedback into performance management can transform the gig team experience:

a). Timely Recognition for Instant Motivation:

Imagine a world where recognition isn't delayed. Real-time feedback allows for instant acknowledgment of a gig worker's contributions. This timely recognition acts as a powerful motivator, fueling a sense of accomplishment and reinforcing positive behaviors.

b). Course Correction on the Fly:

Real-time feedback is like a GPS for gig teams, providing instant course correction. If a project is veering off track or a task needs refinement, immediate feedback allows gig workers to adjust their approach swiftly, ensuring alignment with project goals.

c). Individualized Guidance for Skill Enhancement:

Every gig worker is on a unique professional journey. Real-time feedback enables managers to provide individualized guidance for skill enhancement. It's not just about pointing out areas of improvement; it's about crafting a personalized roadmap for continuous growth.

d). Building a Culture of Open Communication:

Real-time feedback fosters a culture where communication flows openly. It's not a formal performance review; it's a conversation. Encouraging gig workers to share their thoughts, ask questions, and provide feedback in real-time transforms performance management into a collaborative dialogue.

e). Strengthening the Connection to Goals:

In the gig economy, alignment with goals is paramount. Real-time feedback strengthens the connection between individual efforts and overarching objectives. Gig workers can see how their contributions directly impact project success, enhancing their sense of purpose and engagement.

f). Nurturing a Growth Mindset:

Real-time feedback is a catalyst for a growth mindset. It shifts the focus from a fixed performance snapshot to a continuous learning journey. Embracing challenges, learning from mistakes, and evolving professionally become inherent aspects of the gig worker experience.

g). Cultivating Trust and Transparency:

Trust is the bedrock of gig team collaboration. Real-time feedback cultivates trust by promoting transparency. Clear, immediate communication about expectations, progress, and areas for improvement establishes a foundation where gig workers feel valued and supported.

h). Facilitating Peer-to-Peer Recognition:

Real-time feedback isn't solely a top-down process. It opens the door for peer-to-peer recognition. Gig team members can acknowledge each other's efforts instantly, creating a culture where appreciation is not confined to hierarchy but is woven into the fabric of the team.

i). Adapting to Changing Dynamics:

The gig landscape is fluid, and so should be performance management. Real-time feedback allows for adaptability to changing project dynamics, market trends, and client expectations. It's an agile approach to ensuring that performance strategies remain relevant and responsive.

j). Enhancing Employee Experience:

Real-time feedback transforms performance management into an experience. It's not a mere formality; it's a journey of continuous improvement. By enhancing the employee experience, gig workers feel more connected, valued, and empowered in their professional endeavors.

In the tapestry of gig teams, real-time feedback is the thread that weaves together performance, growth, and collaboration. By embracing this approach, performance management becomes a living, breathing entity that adapts, motivates, and propels gig workers toward success in a landscape defined by agility and continuous evolution.

Continuous Learning: HR's Role in Gig Worker Skill Development

In the dynamic landscape of gig work, continuous learning isn't just a nice-to-have; it's the key to unlocking the full potential of gig workers. HR plays a crucial role in orchestrating a continuous learning journey that empowers gig workers to thrive and adapt. Let's delve into the human side of HR's role in gig worker skill development:

a). *Understanding Individual Aspirations*:

HR takes on the role of a career compass. By engaging in conversations with gig workers, understanding their aspirations, and identifying areas of interest, HR tailors learning opportunities that resonate on a personal level. It's about aligning skill development with individual growth journeys.

a). Curating Tailored Learning Paths:

One size rarely fits all in the gig world. HR crafts personalized learning paths that cater to the diverse skills gig workers bring to the table. Whether it's technical skills, soft skills, or industry-specific knowledge, tailoring learning journeys ensures relevance and applicability.

b). Emphasizing Continuous Skill Assessment:

The gig landscape is fluid, and so are the skills required. HR continually assesses the skills landscape, identifying emerging trends and gaps. This ongoing assessment allows for the proactive design of learning initiatives that keep gig workers ahead of the curve.

c). Providing Accessible Learning Resources:

Learning shouldn't be a labyrinth. HR ensures that gig workers have easy access to a plethora of learning resources. Whether it's online courses, webinars, or mentorship programs, providing accessible resources ensures that gig workers can embark on their learning journey seamlessly.

d). Encouraging a Culture of Knowledge Sharing:

Learning is not a solo endeavor; it's a communal experience. HR fosters a culture where gig workers are encouraged to share their knowledge and experiences. This could be through virtual forums, collaborative projects, or mentorship programs that create a symbiotic learning environment.

e). Recognizing and Celebrating Learning Milestones:

Every step in the learning journey is a milestone worth celebrating. HR acknowledges and celebrates gig workers' learning achievements, whether it's completing a course, acquiring a new certification, or mastering a challenging skill. Recognition fuels motivation and a sense of accomplishment.

f). Facilitating Peer Learning Experiences:

Sometimes the most profound learning happens peer-to-peer. HR facilitates opportunities for gig workers to learn from each other through collaborative projects, peer mentoring, or knowledge-sharing sessions. Peer learning creates a vibrant ecosystem of shared expertise.

g). Adapting Learning Initiatives to Project Needs:

HR stays attuned to the requirements of ongoing projects. Learning initiatives are not detached from real-world application; they are intricately woven into the fabric of project needs. This ensures that gig workers acquire skills that directly contribute to project success.

h). Investing in Soft Skills Development:

Beyond technical skills, soft skills are the glue that holds effective gig collaborations together. HR invests in the development of communication, collaboration, and adaptability skills, recognizing that a holistic skill set is pivotal in navigating the gig landscape.

i). Creating a Supportive Learning Culture:

Learning is a journey, not a destination. HR nurtures a supportive learning culture where gig workers feel encouraged to embrace a mindset of continuous improvement. It's about creating an environment where the pursuit of knowledge is not only supported but celebrated.

In the intricate dance of gig work, HR's role in gig worker skill development goes beyond just providing learning opportunities. It's about understanding aspirations, fostering a culture of continuous improvement, and tailoring learning initiatives that resonate on a personal and professional level. By investing in the growth and development of gig workers, HR becomes a catalyst for not just individual success but the overall success of gig projects and the organization.

Adaptive Leadership: Nurturing Agility in HR Professionals

In the ever-evolving landscape of HR, being an adaptive leader is not just a strategy; it's a way of navigating the dynamic currents of change. It's about embracing flexibility, staying attuned to the needs of the workforce, and leading with a human touch. Let's explore the human side of continuous adaptive leadership in HR:

a). Embracing Change as a Constant:

In the realm of HR, change is not a sporadic event; it's a constant companion. Adaptive leaders in HR embrace change as an opportunity for growth rather than a challenge to be overcome. This mindset sets the stage for an agile and resilient HR environment.

b). Listening as a Core Leadership Skill:

Adaptive leadership starts with attentive listening. HR professionals need to be tuned in to the pulse of the workforce, understanding their concerns, aspirations, and evolving needs. Listening creates a foundation of empathy, fostering a culture where the human element is at the forefront.

c). *Learning as a Continuous Journey:*

Adaptive leaders are perpetual learners. They recognize that the world of HR is in a constant state of evolution. Whether it's staying updated on industry trends, technological advancements, or changes in workforce dynamics, continuous learning is ingrained in the fabric of adaptive leadership.

d). *Flexibility in Problem Solving:*

Rigidity rarely serves well in the face of complexity. Adaptive leaders in HR approach problem-solving with flexibility. They understand that solutions need to be as dynamic as the challenges they address, fostering a culture where innovative problem-solving is the norm.

e). *Empowering HR Teams:*

Adaptive leadership is not a solo act; it's a collaborative effort. Adaptive leaders empower HR teams by providing them with the autonomy to make decisions, fostering creativity, and instilling a sense of ownership. Empowered teams become catalysts for adaptive practices.

f). *Anticipating Trends and Challenges:*

Proactive anticipation is a hallmark of adaptive leadership. HR leaders need to be forward-thinking, identifying trends and potential challenges on the horizon. This foresight allows for strategic planning and ensures that HR practices are ahead of the curve.

g). Balancing Data and Intuition:

In the age of analytics, adaptive leaders strike a balance between data-driven decision-making and intuition. They recognize the importance of data but also trust their instincts when navigating uncharted territories. It's a harmonious blend of science and art in leadership.

h). Cultivating Resilience:

Resilience is the armor of adaptive leaders. In the face of setbacks or uncertainties, they model resilience, demonstrating that adaptability is not just about weathering storms but emerging stronger on the other side. This resilience becomes a guiding light for HR teams.

i). Adapting Communication Styles:

Adaptive leaders understand that one size doesn't fit all when it comes to communication. They adapt their communication styles to connect with diverse audiences within the workforce. Effective communication is a bridge that fosters understanding and alignment.

j). Nurturing a Culture of Trust:

Trust is the bedrock of adaptive leadership. HR professionals need to build and nurture a culture of trust, where employees feel confident in the leadership's ability to guide through change. Trust creates a supportive environment that fuels the adaptability of the entire organization.

In the realm of HR, continuous adaptive leadership is a dance of resilience, empathy, and foresight. It's about leading with a human touch, staying agile in the face of change, and fostering an environment where the entire HR ecosystem can flourish. By embodying these principles, HR professionals become not just leaders but architects of a future-ready and people-centric workplace.

8. UNLEASHING POTENTIAL: HR SOLUTIONS FOR A PRODUCTIVE GIG WORKFORCE

In the pulsating realm of the gig workforce, unlocking potential isn't just a goal; it's a strategic imperative. HR professionals stand as architects, poised to craft solutions that go beyond conventional boundaries. "Unleashing Potential: HR Solutions for a Productive Gig Workforce" is not merely a guide; it's a manifesto for redefining how we approach human resources in the dynamic landscape of gig work. Join us in this exploration where HR becomes the catalyst for unleashing untapped talents, fostering innovation, and propelling the gig workforce towards unprecedented productivity.

Employee Engagement in a Virtual World: HR's Guide to Connection

Navigating the virtual realm of work requires HR to be not just guides but architects of connection in a digital landscape. Employee engagement is not just a goal; it's a continuous journey of fostering meaningful connections. Let's explore the human side of HR's guide to connection in the virtual world:

a). Building a Digital Water Cooler:

In the absence of physical office spaces, HR creates a virtual water cooler. Whether it's through chat groups, virtual coffee breaks, or casual video calls, providing spaces for informal interactions fosters a sense of camaraderie and connection.

b). Personalizing Virtual Meetings:

Virtual meetings need a personal touch. HR encourages the human side of virtual interactions—asking about weekends, sharing personal anecdotes, and creating a space where individuals feel seen and valued beyond their professional roles.

c). Celebrating Milestones Virtually:

Birthdays, work anniversaries, or project milestones don't lose their significance in a virtual setting. HR ensures that celebrations transcend physical boundaries, organizing virtual parties, sending digital cards, and making individuals feel cherished, even from afar.

d). Encouraging Open Communication:

Open communication is the lifeline of virtual connections. HR sets the stage for transparent dialogue, encouraging employees to voice their thoughts, concerns, and ideas. An open channel creates a culture of trust and connection.

e). Facilitating Virtual Team Building:

Team building doesn't require physical proximity. HR designs virtual team-building activities that are both engaging and enjoyable. Whether it's online games, virtual escape rooms, or collaborative projects, these activities strengthen the bonds within teams.

f). Creating Virtual Mentorship Programs:

Mentorship doesn't have to be face-to-face. HR establishes virtual mentorship programs, connecting experienced professionals with those seeking guidance. Virtual mentorship transcends geographic constraints, creating valuable connections for professional development.

g). Supporting Employee Well-being:

In a virtual world, well-being takes center stage. HR provides resources and initiatives that support mental and physical well-being. This could include virtual fitness classes, wellness webinars, or mental health support groups, fostering a holistic sense of connection.

h). Fostering Inclusivity in Virtual Spaces:

Inclusivity is pivotal in a digital workspace. HR ensures that virtual meetings are accessible to all, accommodates diverse time zones, and actively promotes an inclusive culture. Every voice, regardless of location, is given space to be heard.

i). Virtual Learning Communities:

HR encourages the formation of virtual learning communities. Whether it's a book club, skill-sharing sessions, or knowledge exchange forums, these communities not only contribute to professional growth but also create bonds among employees with shared interests.

j). Regular Virtual Check-Ins:

Face time matters, even in the virtual realm. HR conducts regular virtual check-ins, not just about work but also about the well-being of employees. These check-ins are a simple yet powerful way to show that HR cares about the people behind the screens.

In the art of connection in a virtual world, HR professionals become the weavers of a digital tapestry where every thread represents a connection, a moment of shared laughter, or a supportive gesture. By prioritizing the human elements of communication, celebration, and well-being, HR guides employees through the virtual landscape, ensuring that the bonds within the team are not just sustained but strengthened in the face of distance.

Holistic Well-being: Integrating Mental Health Support for Gig Workers

In the gig economy, where flexibility and autonomy reign, the well-being of gig workers takes center stage. Integrating mental health support isn't just a policy; it's a commitment to the holistic welfare of individuals navigating the intricate paths of gig work. Let's delve into the human side of holistic well-being and mental health support for gig workers:

a). *Acknowledging the Unique Gig Journey:*

Gig workers embark on a unique professional journey, often marked by highs and lows. Recognizing the individuality of this journey is the first step. HR takes a personalized approach, understanding the nuances of each gig worker's experience and tailoring support accordingly.

b). Creating a Judgment-Free Zone:

Mental health thrives in environments free from judgment. HR fosters a culture where gig workers feel safe sharing their mental health concerns without fear of repercussions. Open conversations reduce stigma, paving the way for proactive support.

c). Flexible Work Arrangements:

Flexibility isn't just about work hours; it extends to mental well-being. HR champions flexible work arrangements that accommodate the ebbs and flows of gig workers' mental health. Whether it's adjusting deadlines or providing time off, flexibility becomes a cornerstone of support.

d). Access to Mental Health Resources:

HR ensures that gig workers have easy access to mental health resources. This could include virtual counseling services, online mental health platforms, or educational materials that empower gig workers to proactively manage their mental well-being.

e). Stress-Reduction Initiatives:

Stress is an inevitable part of gig work. HR introduces stress-reduction initiatives, whether it's mindfulness sessions, virtual yoga classes, or stress management workshops. These initiatives provide practical tools for gig workers to navigate stressors effectively.

f). Regular Check-Ins and Supportive Feedback:

Regular check-ins go beyond project updates; they extend to the well-being of gig workers. HR conducts check-ins that prioritize mental health, creating a space for gig workers to express their concerns, seek advice, or simply share how they're feeling.

g). Empowering with Mental Health Education:

Knowledge is empowering. HR provides gig workers with mental health education, equipping them with an understanding of common mental health challenges and coping mechanisms. This education fosters a proactive approach to mental well-being.

h). Community Building for Peer Support:

Gig workers may operate independently, but they don't have to face mental health challenges alone. HR facilitates the creation of communities where gig workers can connect, share experiences, and provide peer support. This sense of community contributes to a network of mutual understanding.

i). Addressing Burnout and Boundaries:

The risk of burnout is real in gig work. HR addresses this by encouraging gig workers to set boundaries, take breaks, and prioritize self-care. By acknowledging the importance of balance, HR actively works to prevent burnout.

j). Celebrating Achievements, Big and Small:

Mental well-being is also about acknowledging accomplishments. HR celebrates the achievements of gig workers, whether it's completing a challenging project, acquiring new skills, or achieving a personal milestone. Recognition becomes a positive reinforcement of well-being.

In the journey of gig work, where autonomy and self-direction are paramount, HR's role in integrating mental health support is an affirmation of the human side of work. It's about creating a space where gig workers not only thrive professionally but also experience genuine support for their mental well-being. By weaving mental health into the fabric of gig work, HR contributes to a holistic approach that values the people behind the gigs.

HR Technology: Tools for Streamlining Communication in Gig Teams

Navigating the dynamic landscape of gig teams requires more than just coordination; it demands a symphony of seamless communication. In the realm of HR technology, tools emerge as the unsung heroes, orchestrating a harmonious flow of information in gig teams. Let's explore the human side of HR technology—specifically, the tools designed to streamline communication within gig teams:

a). *Unified Communication Platforms:*

HR technology introduces unified communication platforms that act as the central hub for gig teams. These platforms integrate messaging, video conferencing, and file sharing, providing a one-stop-shop for seamless collaboration. It's like having a virtual headquarters where everyone is just a click away.

b). *Real-Time Messaging Apps:*

In the world of gigs, time is of the essence. Real-time messaging apps facilitate instant communication. Whether it's quick project updates, clarifying doubts, or sharing progress, these apps create a digital space where the heartbeat of gig projects is in constant rhythm.

c). Video Conferencing Tools:

Face-to-face interaction, even in a virtual setting, is irreplaceable. Video conferencing tools bring a human touch to digital collaborations. HR technology ensures gig workers can connect, see each other, and build relationships beyond just email exchanges.

d). Project Management Systems:

Gig projects thrive on organization and structure. Project management systems serve as the backbone, providing a collaborative space for task assignment, progress tracking, and milestone achievements. It's the digital blueprint that keeps everyone on the same page.

e). Cloud-Based File Sharing:

The days of email attachments and cumbersome file transfers are behind us. Cloud-based file sharing simplifies document collaboration. HR technology ensures that gig workers can access, edit, and share files seamlessly, fostering a fluid exchange of information.

f). Task Collaboration Boards:

Transparent task management is a hallmark of efficient gig teams. Task collaboration boards provide a visual representation of ongoing tasks, their status, and dependencies. It's akin to a digital whiteboard where everyone can see the collective progress.

g). Chatbots for HR Queries:

Gig workers often have HR-related queries that require swift responses. HR technology integrates chatbots that address common HR questions, from payment inquiries to policy clarifications. It's an instant support system that keeps gig workers informed.

h). Automated Scheduling Tools:

Coordinating across different time zones and schedules is a puzzle. Automated scheduling tools simplify this puzzle, allowing HR professionals to set up meetings, interviews, and collaborative sessions without the back-and-forth struggle.

i). Employee Feedback Platforms:

Feedback is the fuel for improvement. HR technology introduces employee feedback platforms that enable gig workers to share their insights on projects, team collaborations, and overall experiences. It's a digital suggestion box that values every gig worker's perspective.

j). Mobile Apps for On-the-Go Access:

Gig workers are often on the move. HR technology adapts to this reality by providing mobile apps for on-the-go access. Whether it's checking project updates, responding to messages, or accessing HR resources, the tools are within reach wherever gig workers go.

In the realm of gig teams, HR technology becomes the invisible hand that orchestrates communication. These tools are not just about data; they're about human connection, collaboration, and the smooth flow of ideas. By leveraging HR technology in this human-centric way, organizations can empower gig teams to communicate effortlessly and thrive in the digital symphony of modern work.

Maximizing Productivity: Strategies for Remote Gig Employee Success

In the realm of remote gig work, productivity isn't just about meeting deadlines; it's about crafting an environment where gig employees can flourish. The strategies for maximizing productivity in this dynamic setting are as much about human elements as they are about workflow optimization. Let's dive into the human side of strategies for remote gig employee success:

a). Empower with the Right Tools:

Productivity hinges on having the right tools at one's disposal. HR ensures that remote gig employees are equipped with efficient communication platforms, project management tools, and any other technology needed to streamline their workflow. It's about empowering them to work seamlessly from any corner of the world.

b). Flexible Work Schedules:

Acknowledging the diversity of gig workers' lives, HR champions flexible work schedules. Whether it's accommodating different time zones or allowing employees to set their working hours, flexibility becomes a cornerstone of productivity. It's about focusing on outcomes rather than clocking hours.

c). Clear Communication Protocols:

Communication is the backbone of productivity. HR establishes clear communication protocols that include regular updates, transparent project expectations, and guidelines for virtual meetings. Clarity in communication minimizes misunderstandings and keeps everyone aligned.

d). Encourage Regular Breaks:

Productivity isn't a sprint; it's a marathon. HR encourages remote gig employees to take regular breaks. Whether it's a short walk, a coffee break, or a moment of relaxation, breaks contribute to mental well-being and prevent burnout, ultimately enhancing long-term productivity.

e). Virtual Team Building Initiatives:

Despite physical distance, HR initiates virtual team-building activities. Whether it's virtual games, team challenges, or online social events, these initiatives foster a sense of camaraderie among remote gig employees. A connected team is a motivated and productive team.

f). Set Clear Goals and Expectations:

Remote gig employees thrive when they have a clear roadmap. HR collaborates with managers to set transparent goals and expectations. Clarity in objectives ensures that gig workers understand their role in the larger picture and can channel their efforts effectively.

g). Recognition and Feedback:

Recognizing achievements, no matter how small, fuels motivation. HR ensures that remote gig employees receive regular recognition and constructive feedback.

Feeling valued for their contributions is a powerful driver of continued high performance.

h). Provide Learning Opportunities:

Learning is a catalyst for productivity. HR creates avenues for continuous skill development, whether it's through online courses, webinars, or skill-sharing sessions. An empowered gig employee is one who feels their skills are continually evolving.

i). Establish a Supportive Culture:

HR nurtures a culture where remote gig employees feel supported. This involves creating channels for them to voice concerns, seek assistance, or share ideas. A supportive culture fosters trust and a sense of belonging, which are integral to sustained productivity.

j). Encourage Self-Care:

HR actively promotes a culture of self-care. Whether it's through wellness programs, mental health resources, or simply emphasizing the importance of work-life balance, remote gig employees are encouraged to prioritize their well-being. A healthy and balanced individual is a more productive contributor.

In the tapestry of remote gig work, HR's role in maximizing productivity is as much about human-centric strategies as it is about operational efficiency. By focusing on empowerment, clear communication, and fostering a culture of support, HR ensures that remote gig employees not only meet their targets but thrive in a workspace that values their well-being and individual contributions.

9. GIG TALENT ACQUISITION: INNOVATIVE APPROACHES FOR HR PROFESSIONALS

Embarking on the journey of gig talent acquisition requires more than just recruitment; it demands innovation and strategic prowess. In the evolving landscape of work, HR professionals find themselves at the forefront, pioneering new approaches to identify, attract, and retain gig talent. "Gig Talent Acquisition: Innovative Approaches for HR Professionals" isn't just a guide; it's a roadmap for HR leaders navigating the uncharted territories of the gig economy. Join us as we explore groundbreaking strategies, redefine recruitment norms, and unveil the keys to securing top-tier gig talent in a landscape that thrives on agility and ingenuity.

Creative Sourcing: Identifying and Attracting Top Gig Talent

In the world of gig work, identifying and attracting top talent is a bit like curating a unique gallery of skills and expertise. Creative sourcing isn't just about finding candidates; it's about crafting an enticing narrative that draws the best gig talent into the fold. Let's explore the human side of creative sourcing for gig workers:

a). Storytelling in Job Descriptions:

Job descriptions are not just bullet points; they're stories waiting to be told. HR infuses creativity into job descriptions, weaving narratives that showcase the exciting projects, the impact of the role, and the opportunities for growth. It's about making gig opportunities more than just tasks; it's about making them adventures.

b). Highlighting Project Impact:

Top gig talent is drawn to projects that matter. HR emphasizes the impact of each gig opportunity, illustrating how a gig worker's contribution aligns with broader organizational goals. It's about painting a picture of meaningful work that resonates with the aspirations of top talent.

c). Showcasing Company Culture:

Culture isn't confined to office walls. HR creatively showcases the company culture, even in the gig landscape. Whether it's through virtual office tours, employee testimonials, or glimpses into company events, showcasing culture helps top gig talent envision themselves as integral parts of the organization.

d). Engaging Through Social Media:

Social media is the canvas for creative sourcing. HR leverages platforms to engage with potential gig talent authentically. It could be behind-the-scenes glimpses, live Q&A sessions with current gig workers, or sharing success stories. Social media becomes a dynamic tool for building connections.

e). Utilizing Gig Worker Referral Programs:

Gig workers know gig workers. HR establishes referral programs that tap into the networks of current gig employees. This not only brings in potential top talent but also adds a human touch to the recruitment process, as candidates are introduced by colleagues.

f). Interactive Virtual Events:

Traditional job fairs get a virtual makeover. HR organizes interactive virtual events where potential gig talent can engage with company representatives, learn about projects, and get a feel for the organizational culture. It's about creating a digital space for connection.

g). *Personalized Outreach:*

Personalization goes a long way in creative sourcing. HR crafts personalized outreach messages that go beyond generic emails. Understanding the unique skills and experiences of potential gig talent, these messages resonate on a more personal level.

h). *Showcasing Career Progression:*

Gig workers are ambitious; they want to see a path forward. HR creatively showcases career progression opportunities within gig roles. Whether it's through skill development programs, mentorship opportunities, or success stories of gig workers who have advanced, it's about illustrating the potential for growth.

i). *Incorporating Gig Worker Testimonials:*

Nothing speaks louder than the voices of those who have been there. HR incorporates testimonials from current gig workers, sharing their experiences and successes. Authentic voices provide insights that resonate with potential gig talent.

j). Celebrating Diversity and Inclusion:

Diversity isn't just a buzzword; it's a strength. HR creatively communicates the organization's commitment to diversity and inclusion. Highlighting the various perspectives, backgrounds, and experiences within the gig workforce becomes a powerful magnet for top talent.

In the realm of gig talent acquisition, creative sourcing is an art that HR professionals master. It's about understanding that gig workers are not just contributors; they're individuals seeking meaningful experiences and growth opportunities. By infusing creativity into sourcing strategies, HR turns the recruitment process into a vibrant canvas where top gig talent eagerly joins the narrative of the organization.

Tech-Driven Recruitment: Leveraging AI for Gig Worker Matching

In the ever-evolving landscape of gig work, leveraging technology, particularly Artificial Intelligence (AI), is like having a savvy ally in the recruitment journey. It's not just about finding gig workers; it's about orchestrating a symphony of skills and expertise. Let's explore the human side of tech-driven recruitment, where AI becomes the matchmaker connecting organizations with the perfect gig talent:

a). *Understanding Unique Skill Sets:*

AI isn't just crunching numbers; it's deciphering the intricacies of unique skill sets. In tech-driven recruitment, AI dives deep into the pool of data to understand the nuances of gig workers' skills, ensuring a precise match that goes beyond simple keyword matching.

b). *Personalizing Recommendations:*

It's not a one-size-fits-all game. AI personalizes recommendations based on individual preferences, past projects, and the evolving skills of gig workers. It's like having a virtual assistant that understands the distinct characteristics that make each gig worker stand out.

c) Reducing Bias in Selection:

AI becomes a champion in the fight against bias. By focusing on data-driven insights, AI minimizes the impact of unconscious biases, ensuring that gig workers are selected based on merit and skills rather than subjective factors.

d). *Adapting to Evolving Needs:*

The gig landscape is fluid, and so are the needs of organizations. AI adapts to these changes in real-time. Whether it's a sudden shift in project requirements or the emergence of new skills in demand, AI ensures that gig worker matching stays agile.

e). *Enhancing the Candidate Experience:*

Tech-driven recruitment isn't just about the employer; it's about the gig worker experience too. AI streamlines the application process, provides instant feedback, and offers a seamless interface, contributing to a positive and efficient candidate experience.

f). *Ensuring Cultural Fit:*

It's not just about skills; it's about fitting into the organizational culture. AI incorporates cultural fit indicators, analyzing past collaborations, and aligning gig workers with environments where they are likely to thrive.

g). *Facilitating Skill Development Paths:*

AI doesn't just stop at matching current skills; it maps out potential skill development paths. By identifying gaps and recommending relevant training or upskilling opportunities, AI becomes a guide in the continuous growth journey of gig workers.

h). *Sourcing from Diverse Talent Pools:*

Diversity is a strength, and AI actively sources from diverse talent pools. It broadens the scope, ensuring that organizations have access to a rich tapestry of skills and perspectives within the gig workforce.

i). *Creating Transparent Processes:*

Trust is the foundation of successful gig collaborations. AI contributes to transparency by providing clear insights into the matching process. Gig workers understand the criteria used, ensuring that the process is not shrouded in mystery.

j). *Humanizing the Tech Interface:*

Behind every algorithm is a human story. AI-human collaboration becomes the essence of tech-driven recruitment. While AI handles the data crunching, HR professionals bring in the human touch—understanding aspirations, providing mentorship, and ensuring that gig workers feel seen and valued.

In the dance of tech-driven recruitment, AI emerges not as a replacement for human intuition but as an enabler. It's a tool that amplifies the capabilities of HR professionals, allowing them to focus on the human elements of the gig worker experience. Together, AI and HR professionals create a dynamic partnership that ensures organizations find not just gig workers but collaborators who bring unique value to the projects at hand.

Interviewing Virtually: Adapting HR Practices for Remote Hiring

As our professional landscapes continue to evolve, so do the strategies for finding the right talent. Interviewing virtually isn't just a contingency plan; it's a skill, an art, and a necessity in the era of remote hiring. Let's explore the human side of adapting HR practices for virtual interviews:

a). Creating a Welcoming Virtual Space:

A virtual interview isn't just about questions and answers; it's about creating a welcoming environment. HR professionals set the stage by ensuring that the virtual space is well-lit, distraction-free, and that both interviewer and candidate feel comfortable.

b). Building Connection from Afar:

Connecting virtually goes beyond the screen. HR professionals understand the importance of building rapport. Small talk, sharing a bit about the company culture, or even discussing shared interests—these become the threads that weave a connection in the digital space.

c). Setting Expectations Clearly:

Virtual interviews come with their own set of nuances. HR ensures that expectations are communicated clearly—from the format of the interview to any technical requirements. This clarity sets the tone for a smooth and stress-free virtual meeting.

d). Embracing Video for a Personal Touch:

While emails and phone calls have their place, video adds a personal touch. HR encourages video interviews to bridge the gap, allowing both parties to see facial expressions, body language, and create a more human connection.

e). Adapting to Technical Glitches with Grace:

Technology is wonderful when it works, but glitches happen. HR professionals approach technical issues with grace, understanding that these are part of the virtual landscape. A patient and understanding demeanor during such moments reflects the human side of remote interviewing.

f). Incorporating Interactive Elements:

Interviews aren't monologues; they're dialogues. HR introduces interactive elements to keep the conversation engaging. This could include virtual whiteboards for problem-solving, collaborative documents, or even a quick tour of the virtual office.

g). Focusing on Candidate Experience:

The candidate experience remains at the heart of HR practices. HR professionals actively seek feedback from candidates about their virtual interview experience, ensuring that improvements can be made to continually enhance the process.

h). Tailoring Questions for Virtual Dynamics:

The questions asked in a virtual interview may differ from those in a traditional setting. HR professionals tailor questions to assess not just skills but also a candidate's ability to navigate virtual collaboration, communication, and remote work dynamics.

i). Providing Opportunities for Q&A:

Virtual interviews are a two-way street. HR ensures that candidates have ample opportunities to ask questions. This not only helps them gather information but also signals that their perspective is valued in the hiring process.

j). Following Up Promptly and Personally:

The virtual space doesn't diminish the importance of personal touches. HR professionals follow up promptly after virtual interviews, providing feedback and insights. This personalized touch reinforces the human connection established during the interview.

In the realm of virtual interviews, HR practices become a delicate dance of technology and humanity. It's about leveraging the efficiency of virtual platforms while ensuring that the human touch isn't lost. By adapting practices to the unique dynamics of remote hiring, HR professionals play a pivotal role in not just finding the right talent but in creating a positive and engaging experience for candidates.

Building a Gig-Ready Pipeline: Proactive Talent Acquisition Strategies

Building a gig-ready pipeline is not just about filling roles; it's about cultivating a dynamic ecosystem where talent flows seamlessly. In the world of gig work, where flexibility and agility are paramount, HR professionals play the role of architects, shaping strategies that anticipate needs and connect with the right gig talent. Let's explore the human side of proactive talent acquisition for building a gig-ready pipeline:

a). Understanding Gig Worker Aspirations:

Beyond just skill sets, HR delves into the aspirations of gig workers. What projects excite them? What skills are they eager to develop? By understanding the human side of gig aspirations, HR can align opportunities with individual career goals.

b). Fostering a Network of Relationships:

Talent acquisition isn't a one-time transaction; it's about building relationships. HR professionals actively foster a network of relationships with gig workers, freelancers, and contractors. This network becomes the foundation for a robust gig-ready pipeline.

c). Emphasizing Continuous Communication:

Proactivity begins with communication. HR establishes channels for continuous communication with potential gig talent. Whether through newsletters, updates on upcoming projects, or periodic check-ins, the dialogue is ongoing and meaningful.

d). Showcasing the Gig Work Experience:

The gig work experience is not just a job; it's a journey. HR creatively showcases success stories, testimonials, and highlights from previous gig workers. This storytelling adds a human touch, allowing potential talent to envision themselves as integral parts of the gig ecosystem.

e). Offering Learning and Development Opportunities:

Gig workers are drawn to opportunities for growth. HR introduces learning and development initiatives tailored for gig talent. Whether it's skill-building webinars, access to online courses, or mentorship programs, these opportunities make the gig proposition even more enticing.

f). Creating a Transparent Gig Culture:

Transparency is the cornerstone of a gig-ready culture. HR ensures that the expectations, project details, and collaboration dynamics are communicated transparently. This openness fosters trust, making gig workers more inclined to be part of the pipeline.

g). Proactively Identifying Skill Gaps:

Anticipation is key in proactive talent acquisition. HR identifies potential skill gaps in upcoming projects and actively seeks gig workers with those specific skills. This foresight ensures that the pipeline is ready to meet the evolving needs of the organization.

h). Leveraging Talent Pools Effectively:

Talent pools are not static; they're dynamic reservoirs of potential. HR leverages talent pools effectively by regularly assessing skills, preferences, and availability.

This active management ensures that the gig-ready pipeline is agile and responsive.

i). Facilitating Seamless Onboarding Processes:

A smooth onboarding experience sets the tone for the gig journey. HR streamlines onboarding processes, ensuring that gig workers feel supported, informed, and connected from day one. The onboarding experience becomes a crucial touchpoint for building a positive relationship.

j). Gathering and Acting on Feedback:

The gig-ready pipeline is a collaborative effort. HR actively seeks feedback from gig workers—whether it's about the recruitment process, project experiences, or suggestions for improvement. This feedback loop ensures continuous refinement and enhancement of the talent acquisition strategy.

In the realm of gig-ready talent acquisition, HR professionals become the architects of a living, breathing ecosystem. It's about understanding the human nuances of gig work, fostering relationships, and creating an environment where gig talent doesn't just contribute but thrives. By proactively anticipating needs, communicating openly, and embracing a culture of continuous improvement, HR builds a gig-ready pipeline that not only meets the current demands but also evolves in sync with the dynamic nature of gig work.

10. HR'S GIG GUIDE: NAVIGATING EMPLOYMENT TRENDS IN A FLEXIBLE WORLD

In the ever-shifting landscape of employment trends, HR professionals emerge as navigators, guiding organizations through the intricate paths of a flexible world. "HR's Gig Guide: Navigating Employment Trends in a Flexible World" is not merely a handbook; it's a compass for HR leaders steering through the dynamic currents of contemporary work structures. Join us on this journey as we explore the nuances of gig employment, decode trends, and chart a course for HR strategies that resonate with the pulse of flexibility in today's ever-evolving professional landscape.

Keeping Pace with Change: HR's Continuous
Learning in Gig Trends

In the fast-paced world of gig trends, HR isn't just a conductor orchestrating talent; it's a perpetual learner, always tuned into the evolving rhythms of the gig economy. Staying ahead involves more than just tracking trends; it's about continuous learning, adaptation, and a genuine embrace of change. Let's delve into the human side of HR's journey in keeping pace with gig trends:

a). Embracing a Growth Mindset:

Continuous learning begins with mindset. HR professionals cultivate a growth mindset, viewing challenges as opportunities for learning and evolution. It's an attitude that not only adapts to change but actively seeks it as a catalyst for improvement.

b). Curating a Personalized Learning Journey:

The gig landscape is diverse, and so are the skills needed. HR doesn't just follow generic learning paths; it curates personalized journeys for continuous skill development. Whether it's through online courses, industry conferences, or mentorship programs, the focus is on relevance to the gig ecosystem.

c). Building Networks and Communities:

Learning thrives in communities. HR actively participates in and builds networks of professionals connected to the gig economy. This could be through industry forums, social media groups, or collaborative platforms where insights and experiences are shared.

d). Staying Current with Industry Insights:

The gig economy is a dynamic tapestry of trends. HR professionals immerse themselves in industry insights, regularly reading publications, attending webinars, and participating in discussions to stay current. It's about understanding not just where the gig economy is but where it's heading.

e). Experimenting with New Technologies:

Technology shapes the future of work. HR doesn't shy away from experimenting with new tools and platforms that enhance recruitment, management, and collaboration within gig teams. It's about being hands-on with technology to better understand its impact on gig trends.

f). Encouraging Cross-Functional Learning:

Silos are the antithesis of agility. HR fosters cross-functional learning, encouraging professionals to gain insights beyond their traditional roles. Understanding how different facets of the organization operate contributes to a holistic understanding of gig trends.

g). Seeking Feedback and Iterating:

Feedback is the compass in the journey of continuous learning. HR actively seeks feedback from gig workers, other HR professionals, and industry experts. This iterative process ensures that HR strategies adapt in real-time to the changing dynamics of the gig landscape.

h). Prioritizing Soft Skills Development:

In the gig economy, soft skills are the currency of collaboration. HR places a premium on soft skills development, recognizing the importance of communication, adaptability, and emotional intelligence in managing gig teams effectively.

i). Navigating Legal and Compliance Changes:

The legal landscape of gig work evolves. HR professionals proactively engage with legal and compliance updates, ensuring that their strategies align with the ever-changing regulatory environment. This proactive approach mitigates risks and maintains a compliant gig ecosystem.

j). Cultivating a Culture of Continuous Learning:

Learning isn't an event; it's a culture. HR instills a culture of continuous learning within the organization, encouraging all employees to embrace the mindset of perpetual growth. This cultural shift ensures that everyone, from HR professionals to gig workers, is invested in staying ahead of the curve.

In the symphony of gig trends, HR professionals become not just observers but active participants. It's about recognizing that staying ahead isn't a one-time effort but a perpetual journey of adaptation, curiosity, and a commitment to understanding the nuances of the gig economy. By embracing continuous learning, HR not only keeps pace with change but becomes a driving force in shaping the future of work.

Collaborative Platforms: HR's Role in Facilitating Gig Team Interaction

In the realm of gig work, where collaboration knows no physical boundaries, HR steps in as the orchestrator of team dynamics on virtual stages. Collaborative platforms become the beating heart of gig team interaction, and HR takes center stage in ensuring that these platforms aren't just tools but vibrant spaces for human connection. Let's delve into the human side of HR's role in facilitating gig team interaction on collaborative platforms:

a). Choosing Platforms with a Human Touch:

HR isn't just picking software; it's selecting platforms that resonate with the human experience. Whether it's a project management tool or a communication platform, HR ensures that the chosen tools prioritize user-friendly interfaces and intuitive features that enhance, not hinder, collaboration.

b). Fostering a Sense of Community:

Collaboration isn't just about tasks; it's about community. HR actively fosters a sense of belonging within gig teams. This involves creating virtual spaces for team discussions, informal chats, and even virtual watercooler moments. It's about recreating the camaraderie of an office setting in the digital realm.

c). Promoting Open Communication Channels:

HR ensures that communication isn't confined to emails. Collaborative platforms become a canvas for open channels where gig team members can freely share ideas, ask questions, and engage in real-time discussions. The emphasis is on breaking down communication barriers and fostering transparency.

d). Encouraging Virtual Collaboration Rituals:

Just like in an office, rituals add a human touch. HR encourages virtual collaboration rituals—whether it's a weekly video check-in, a virtual Friday coffee meetup, or shared playlists. These rituals create a sense of continuity and shared experiences within the gig team.

e). Providing Training and Support:

Not everyone is a tech wizard, and that's okay. HR provides training and support to gig team members, ensuring that everyone is comfortable navigating collaborative platforms. This proactive approach minimizes the learning curve and promotes confidence in using these tools effectively.

f). Understanding Team Dynamics:

HR isn't just monitoring tasks; it's understanding the dynamics of the gig team. This involves recognizing individual strengths, acknowledging potential conflicts, and tailoring collaborative approaches that suit the unique composition of the team.

g). Celebrating Milestones and Achievements:

Recognition is a powerful motivator. HR actively celebrates milestones and achievements within the gig team. Whether it's completing a project, achieving a significant milestone, or even a simple shout-out for a job well done, acknowledgment becomes a cornerstone of team interaction.

h). Integrating Feedback Loops:

Collaboration is a two-way street. HR establishes feedback loops on collaborative platforms, providing a channel for gig team members to share their thoughts on the platforms used, communication processes, and overall team dynamics. It's about creating a space for continuous improvement.

i). Addressing Challenges Proactively:

Challenges are inevitable, especially in virtual collaborations. HR takes a proactive approach in addressing challenges, whether they involve technical issues with platforms or interpersonal conflicts within the team. Swift and empathetic resolutions contribute to a positive team environment.

j). Ensuring Inclusivity in Digital Spaces:

In the digital realm, inclusivity takes intentional efforts. HR ensures that collaborative platforms are inclusive spaces where every gig team member has equal opportunities to contribute. This involves creating guidelines for virtual meetings, providing accessibility features, and actively promoting a culture of respect.

In the world of gig team interaction, HR becomes the guardian of the virtual realm. It's not just about managing tasks; it's about curating an environment where gig team members feel connected, supported, and valued. By infusing collaborative platforms with a human touch, HR transforms digital spaces into lively hubs where the essence of teamwork thrives, transcending the boundaries of physical distance.

Predictive Analytics: Anticipating HR Needs in the Gig Economy

In the intricate dance of the gig economy, HR takes on the role of a forward-thinking choreographer, and predictive analytics becomes the spotlight that illuminates the path ahead. It's not just about managing the present; it's about anticipating HR needs and orchestrating strategies that harmonize with the dynamic nature of gig work. Let's explore the human side of HR's journey in leveraging predictive analytics for the gig economy:

a). Understanding the Symphony of Skills:

Predictive analytics in HR begins with understanding the nuanced symphony of skills in the gig economy. It's not just about the technical; it's about predicting the evolving landscape of skills that gig workers bring to the table. HR delves into data to anticipate what skills will be in demand tomorrow.

b). *Mapping the Rhythms of Talent Supply and Demand:*

The gig economy is a pulsating ecosystem of supply and demand. HR uses predictive analytics to map these rhythms—identifying peak periods of demand for certain skills, understanding when talent may be scarce, and proactively preparing for these fluctuations.

c). *Forecasting Project Requirements:*

Anticipation extends to project needs. Predictive analytics enables HR to forecast project requirements accurately. Whether it's the number of gig workers needed, the specific skill sets required, or the optimal duration of engagements, HR aligns resources with the anticipated demands of upcoming projects.

d). *Identifying Skill Gaps in Advance:*

Skill gaps can be stumbling blocks in the gig economy. HR leverages predictive analytics to identify potential skill gaps in advance. By understanding the evolving needs of projects and the skill trajectories of gig workers, HR can proactively address gaps through training or targeted recruitment.

e). *Enhancing Retention Strategies:*

Predictive analytics isn't just about bringing talent in; it's about keeping it within the fold. HR anticipates factors that contribute to gig worker retention. This involves understanding the drivers of job satisfaction, predicting potential attrition risks, and crafting retention strategies that align with gig workers' expectations.

f). Optimizing Talent Pools:

Talent pools are not static; they're dynamic reservoirs waiting to be optimized. HR uses predictive analytics to optimize talent pools—identifying high-potential gig workers, understanding their preferences, and strategically placing them within the organization's gig-ready pipeline.

g). Creating Personalized Learning Paths:

The gig economy thrives on continuous learning. Predictive analytics assists HR in creating personalized learning paths for gig workers. By analyzing historical data and understanding individual skill trajectories, HR tailors learning opportunities that align with the unique growth journeys of gig workers.

h). Anticipating Compliance and Legal Needs:

The legal landscape of gig work is ever-evolving. HR utilizes predictive analytics to anticipate compliance and legal needs. This involves staying ahead of regulatory changes, understanding potential legal challenges, and ensuring that HR practices align with the shifting legal landscape.

i). Strategizing Compensation and Benefits:

Compensation isn't just a number; it's a strategy. Predictive analytics aids HR in strategizing compensation and benefits packages for gig workers. By analyzing market trends, industry benchmarks, and individual performance data, HR ensures that compensation remains competitive and enticing.

j). Aligning HR Strategies with Organizational Goals:

Predictive analytics in HR is not a standalone endeavor; it's about aligning strategies with broader organizational goals. HR uses predictive insights to ensure that talent acquisition, retention, and development strategies are in sync with the overarching objectives of the organization in the dynamic gig landscape.

In the realm of predictive analytics, HR becomes a navigator, steering the ship through the ever-changing currents of the gig economy. It's about harnessing data not just for insights but for crafting proactive strategies that anticipate the needs, aspirations, and challenges of gig workers. By combining the art of human understanding with the science of predictive analytics, HR doesn't just respond to the gig economy; it shapes it with foresight and agility.

The Future of Work: Shaping HR Practices in an Evolving Landscape

In the ever-evolving landscape of work, HR professionals find themselves at the forefront of change, donning the dual hats of architects and navigators. The future of work isn't a distant horizon; it's a dynamic canvas being painted with each innovation and shift in the professional landscape. Let's delve into the human side of HR practices, where adaptability, empathy, and a keen understanding of evolving trends shape the future of work:

a). Embracing Remote Work Realities:

The future of work is no longer tethered to desks; it's about embracing the realities of remote work. HR adapts practices to create environments where virtual collaboration is seamless, employees feel connected irrespective of location, and the workday is redefined beyond traditional boundaries.

b). Prioritizing Employee Well-being:

Beyond the confines of office walls, HR places a premium on employee well-being. Mental health, work-life balance, and holistic well-being take center stage. The future workplace isn't just about productivity metrics; it's about creating spaces where employees thrive both professionally and personally.

c). Fostering Inclusive Cultures:

Diversity isn't just a checkbox; it's a strength. HR practices evolve to foster inclusive cultures where every voice is heard and valued. The future workplace thrives on the richness of perspectives, backgrounds, and experiences that contribute to a vibrant tapestry of innovation.

d). Nurturing Continuous Learning:

The future of work is a journey of perpetual learning. HR cultivates environments where continuous learning isn't a choice but a culture. From upskilling programs to personalized learning paths, HR practices become catalysts for empowering employees to navigate the evolving demands of their roles.

e). Adopting Agile Talent Management:

Flexibility isn't just a buzzword; it's a strategy. HR embraces agile talent management practices, allowing organizations to pivot swiftly in response to changing priorities. The future workplace is about agility—whether it's adapting to market shifts, project demands, or unforeseen challenges.

f). Leveraging Technology Thoughtfully:

Technology isn't just a tool; it's a companion in the future workplace. HR practices involve leveraging technology thoughtfully—whether it's AI for talent acquisition, collaborative platforms for virtual teamwork, or data analytics for informed decision-making.

g). Facilitating Hybrid Work Models:

The future workplace is a blend of physical and virtual realms. HR pioneers hybrid work models that offer flexibility without compromising collaboration. It's about creating environments where employees can choose the work mode that aligns with their preferences and tasks.

h). Building Resilient Teams:

Resilience is not just a personal trait nor quality; it is a team characteristic. HR practices focus on building resilient teams that can weather uncertainties. This involves fostering a culture of adaptability, providing support structures, and instilling a sense of collective purpose.

i). Aligning HR Strategies with Business Goals:

The future of work isn't a standalone concept; it's intricately tied to organizational goals. HR practices align with business objectives, ensuring that talent strategies are synchronized with the broader vision of the company in a rapidly evolving professional landscape.

j). Cultivating Empathetic Leadership:

Leadership isn't just about directives; it's about empathy. HR actively cultivates empathetic leadership practices where leaders understand and respond to the diverse needs of their teams. In the future workplace, leadership isn't a top-down approach; it's a collaborative journey.

In the tapestry of the future workplace, HR professionals wield brushes of adaptability, empathy, and strategic vision. It's about understanding that the future isn't a fixed destination but a journey of continuous evolution. By shaping HR practices to align with the human nuances of work—whether remote, hybrid, or in traditional settings—HR becomes the cornerstone in crafting a future of work that is not just productive but also deeply human and fulfilling.

11. CONCLUSION

As we draw the final curtain on "Human Resource in the Gig Economy," the journey through the dynamic landscapes of the gig workforce comes to a momentary pause. Authored by Eugene George A., this book has been a compass, guiding HR professionals through the uncharted territories of a rapidly evolving professional realm.

In our exploration, we've delved into the intricacies of talent management in a gig-driven world, dissecting the challenges and opportunities that define the future of work. Eugene George A. has artfully unveiled strategies, innovative approaches, and practical insights that resonate with the pulsating rhythm of the gig economy.

The gig workforce isn't a mere trend; it's a paradigm shift in how we perceive and engage with work. As we navigate this landscape, HR professionals find themselves not just as guardians of traditional practices but as architects of change, crafting agile strategies that mirror the flexibility demanded by the modern workforce.

From the corridors of talent acquisition to the boardrooms of leadership, this book has provided a roadmap for HR leaders, emphasizing the human side of HR practices in the gig era. It's not just about policies and procedures; it's about understanding the unique aspirations, challenges, and potential of the gig workers who define this new world of work.

As we close this chapter, let these insights be not just conclusions but catalysts for action. The future of work is not stagnant; it's a canvas awaiting the strokes of innovative HR practices. Eugene George A. has ignited a spark—an invitation to HR professionals to be the pioneers, the visionaries, and the architects of a future where the gig economy isn't just navigated but actively shaped.

In the ever-evolving symphony of work, may "Human Resource in the Gig Economy" be your guide, empowering you to navigate the future world of work with wisdom, agility, and a deep understanding of the human dynamics that propel the gig economy forward. As we bid adieu to these pages, let them be an echo, a reminder that HR's role isn't just in adapting to change; it's in orchestrating a future where work is not just a destination but a dynamic journey of innovation and possibility.

REFERENCE

1. Mulcahy, D. (2015). *The Gig Economy: A Complete Guide to Getting Better Work, Taking More Time Off, and Financing the Life You Want.*

2. Ulrich, D., & Younger, J. (2012). *HR from the Outside In: Six Competencies for the Future of Human Resource.*

3. Morgan, J. (2014). *The Future of Work: Attract New Talents, Build Better Leaders, and Create a Competitive Organizations.*

4. Dessler, G. (2019). *Human Resource Management.*

5. Bhatia, T. (2018). *The Lean HR: Changing the HR Game and Making it Lean.*

6. Hoffman, R., Casnocha, B., & Yeh, C. (2014). *The Alliance: Managing Talent in the Networked Age.*

7. Boudreau, J. W., & Cascio, W. F. (2017). *Reimagining HR: A New Competitive Agenda for the Digital Era.* Harvard Business Review Press.

8. Raman, A., & Osterman, P. (2018). *Organizing and Reorganizing: Power and Change in U.S. Labor Unions.* ILR Press.

9. Schramm, J. (2019). *Burn the Business Plan: What Great Entrepreneurs Really Do.* Simon & Schuster.

10. Davenport, T. H., Harris, J., & Shapiro, J. (2010). *Competing on Analytics: The New Sciences of Winning.* Harvard Business Press.

11. Pink, D. H. (2018). *When: The Scientific Secrets of Perfect Timing.* Riverhead Books.

12. Cappelli, P.S (2019). *Why Good People Can't Get Jobs: The Skill Gap and What Companies Can Do About It.* Public Affairs.